A Girl with Tangled Hair

AHA Books

ISBN-13:978-0944676547

ISBN-10:0944676545

AHA Books
P.O. Box 767
Gualala, CA 95445
USA

Jane@AHApoetry.com
www.AHApoetry.com

A Girl with Tangled Hair

**The 399 tanka in *Midaregami – Tangled Hair*
by Akiko Yosano**

Translated by
Jane Reichhold
and
Machiko Kobayashi

CONTENTS

INTRODUCTION

Radiance Beyond a Century
by Aya Yuhki

It has long been Jane Reichhold's dream to translate Akiko Yosano's collection of tanka, *Tangled Hair*, into English. Jane first began working with Hatsue Kawamura when the first issue of the *Tanka Journal* was published by the Japan Tanka Poets' Society in 1992.

Together they selected, translated, and published 100 tanka from the collections of Fumi Saito, Akiko Baba, and Fumiko Nakajo. Jane also worked closely with Hatsue in the translation of the tanka songs included in the *Tale of Genji*. Jane once said to me that through her work with Hatsue she began to understand and appreciate Japanese tanka.

Generally speaking, the literature of a country is the result of its innate language, culture and environment. Tanka, a traditional fixed-form style of poetry, has lasted more than 1,300 years, and continues to be the backbone of Japanese literature. It may even be considered unique amongst the many forms of poetry.

Several years ago, Hatsue fell into a coma. This very unfortunate event left Jane without a close friend and translation partner. In 2010 the International Pen Club Congress was held in Tokyo and Jane was invited to lecture on tanka. It was here, during a meeting with our members of the *Tanka Journal*, that she met a translator by the name of Michiko Kobayashi. This would prove to be a defining moment in the success of this book.

They immediately started translating one tanka a day and did so for more than a year. Akiko Yosano's tanka, in her *Tangled Hair* collection, freely and boldly expresses the passion of love, containing many ambiguous expressions. As a result, they are difficult to understand clearly, even for us Japanese.

As you know, the structure of sentences in English is rather fixed. For example, a normal sentence includes a subject and a verb, so distinguishing between singular and plural is essential.

This is not the case in Japanese. In fact, we often omit the subject and sometimes do not pay much attention to the difference between "a tree" or "many trees." You can easily imagine how challenging this makes it to translate even the simplest tanka poem, let alone those in *Tangled Hair*.

It is also important to consider the context in which the tanka was written. The more background you have to a tanka — the characters involved and the conditions it was written under, for example — the more you can really appreciate it. Because tanka is a small vessel of only 31 sound units the context can be useful. This book aims to give readers just that kind of information.

Knowing the background to the complicated love affairs surrounding Tekkan helps us, as the readers, to a better understanding of Akiko's tanka. As for the interpretations of Japanese habits, customs and flora, perhaps they could on occasion be briefer for some readers.

Initially, I wondered why Jane felt so compelled to throw all her passion into a complete translation of every tanka in *Tangled Hair*. After all, the book was published more than a century ago and has already been partially translated into English by Jannie Beichman, an expert researcher into Japanese literature. But after reading this book, I am able to understand the motivation more clearly.

After World War II, we Japanese women were given equal rights to men. Nowadays women can love and marry of their own will, without the need for their parents' permission. But those rights, as it were, were given to us as a result of the end of war and the sudden arrival of new ideas on Japanese shores. The tendency towards women's liberation in 1960s and 1970s promoted and fostered ideals of freedom.

In comparison, in Akiko's time there was no wind of social change. Akiko, only twenty years old at that time, listened to her inner voice and tried to be entirely faithful to her feelings and thoughts. She was unaware that, through her enthusiasm for Tekkan and tanka, she was starting down the road of women's freedom and independence. Akiko believed that to express her true emotions was the only way to struggle with many undesirable aspects of her reality.

At this point, I feel it is important to note that she came from a family of merchants in the city of Sakai. In the time of the Edo Period, the *Daimyo* — Japanese feudal lords — depended greatly on these wealthy merchants. Consequently, the city experienced unusual freedoms and became a flourishing guild city. Akiko supposedly inherited the powerful traits that came from Sakai merchants.

Jane is able to identify, and perceive, through her intuition as a poet, Akiko's inner flare and to interpret her energy for life. I deeply respect Jane's poetic sensitivity and insight. Let's take a look at some of Akiko's tanka.

40
tangled feelings
among puzzled feelings
so often
the god tramples on the lily
since bare breasts aren't covered

321
spring is short
so what remains in life
that is everlasting
I let his hands grope for
my powerful breasts

This was the first time in the long history of Japanese tanka that a woman expressed her sensual feelings so boldly. We find similar such lines in many other tanka of *Tangled Hair*.

2
ask among poems
who denies a bright red
to field flowers
a girl is also attractive
with her sin of scarlet

143
is it sin
to let him rest
on my arm pillow?
its pale skin
is the gift of god?

As the two tanka above demonstrate, Akiko creates a romantic yet painful image caused by the struggle between the consciousness of her sin and the pleasure of her love. I imagine this is the reason why the readers at the time felt such sympathy for Akiko.

6
the girl is twenty
her hair is a black stream
running through a comb
in spring even pride
is beautiful

352
not preaching
not thinking of the future
nor asking for fame
here I only see
you and I in love

Akiko was aware that it was arrogant to give priority to love, but her pure passion transcends her self-consciousness. This is why she was able to attract readers not only of her time, but also those of today.

75
a vague feeling
you are waiting for me
I go out
in a flowering field
on a moonlit evening

237
I pick wild roses
some for my hair
others in my hand
struggling the long day
waiting for you in a field

These two tanka describe a woman waiting for her lover, a common theme throughout the tradition of tanka. *Tangled Hair* includes several such songs. In ancient times, long black hair was a symbol of an attractive woman and among the many tanka which describe hair I would like to quote one I feel relates to the title of this book:

260
black hair
a thousand strands of hair
tangled
disturbed my heart
tangled with memories

The work of translation is delicate, especially in the field of poetry. Considering this, it is splendid that, with the help of Machiko Kobayashi, the reading of every tanka is so beautifully accurate. Machiko's reading and Jane's technique come together to form exquisite tanka poems. It is with great pleasure that I recommend this book to all who love tanka.

NOTES ON TRANSLATIONS

First of all I want to express my thanks to Machiko for being, not only a first-rate translator, but also a marvelous person. Her competence, attention to detail and willingliness to work were simply amazing. She was a joy to correspond with and we shared so much about tanka, life and ourselves that I shall never forget the experience. My deepest gratitude to Machiko for taking on the job, somewhat out of her line, and for doing it so well and with such pleasure.

TANKA / WAKA

Waka are what we now call tanka. When poems were first written down, in 760 CE they were called *uta* – songs. Gradually the ones written in five sections containing 5, 7, 5, 7, 7, sound units or *kana* were called waka. Then the term *tanka* – short elegance was substituted. Now only the poems by the Imperial Family are called *waka*. The rest of us, and English speakers, use the term tanka.

Tanka are the oldest poetry form still in use. You can find the same poem format in the earliest stories of the cosmetology of Japan and it is featured in the oldest anthology of Japanese poetry – *Man'yōshu* – *A Myriad Leaves,* and even more so in the imperial anthologies that followed. Though the popularity of tanka writing rose and fell, to be replaced at times with renga, and haiku, it is still the most used poetry form in Japan and is finally spreading around the world in the wake of the better-known haiku.

Haiku are shorter than tanka, containing only the upper part of a tanka, and traditionally more objective. The two extra lines of tanka allow for the expression of subjective matters – the feelings of the poet. Thus, while most haiku masters are men, throughout the ages it has been the women who excelled in writing tanka.

There should be a leap in meaning, or a change in voice, mood, place, or person, between the two halves of a tanka. Very often there is a mention of the natural world as it compares or associates or contrasts with the human feelings that builds this relationship. In English typography the five units of the tanka are placed in five lines. Since the original tanka is written in sentence fragments and phrases – not on-going sentences – the modern method of writing tanka drops all the capital letters at the beginning of a line and since the line ends automatically form pauses, even punctuation is not needed. This allows more ambiguity and changes in meaning – the foundations of tanka.

NAMES
The Japanese custom is to give first the family name and then the personal or what we call the first name. I have decided to give names the English order so the reader, when talking about the people in the book in English with others, will be accustomed to recognizing the name.

REASONS FOR THIS BOOK
Due to the popularity of Akiko Yosano's book, *Midaregami – Tangled Hair* several poets and translators have published their selections of tanka put into English. However, until now there has not been a translation of all the tanka in the original book. In this translation are the 399 poems kept in the original order of the first edition. This allows the reader to appreciate, and study, how Akiko compiled her work. Janine Beichman, in her deep and professional study of all of Akiko Yosano's work – *Embracing the Firebird*, makes the case that Akiko used renga methods of linking her works. It was my goal to read all the poems in English to see if I agreed. I don't, but the journey has been more exciting than the arrival. As a tanka poet I have learned so much from working with Akiko's poems. I hope this will be true for others. I also hope that persons working in translation will find delight in translating these small poems as exercise of new word skills.

One of the devices Akiko Yosano used in her tanka was direct speech. Instead of showing this with quotation marks, as is normal in English, we had chosen to use italics.

The original book was composed of secquences and these are used in the translation also.

There is an art in reading tanka – how to let one's mind leap and switch meaning between the lines – so we hope we have given you enough help so you can have this experience.

Jane Reichhold
Gualala, CA
July, 2013

THE BOOK *Midaregami – Tangled Hair*

Though Akiko Yosano had studied both haiku and tanka and had some of her early tanka published in magazines, it was only after coming under the influence of Tekkan Yosano, reading his magazine *Myōjō – Morning Star or Bright Star* – and finally meeting him that she achieved a new freedom in her poetry. He encouraged her, not to follow the current tanka rules and subject matter, but to express only what she was feeling in her tanka. This was hard for her to accept and understand so she asked him several times if she could really do this.

Tekkan had been a proponent of this idea for several years, encouraging male writers to be more masculine, to be themselves, to write "tiger" tanka. He called his movement "The New Poetry Society" of which *Myōjō* was the publication to promote their works. Tekkan made trips out of Tokyo to Kyoto and Osaka to hold workshops to teach his new ideas.

This was how he met Akiko – at one of his workshops. Very early he recognized that she was not like the others in his group. Through her comments and her early tanka written in his style, he saw what a very strong talent she was. No one else had taken his ideas in so completely and was able to so quickly turn them into tanka.

Tekkan was able to encourage her by publishing her poems almost as soon as she wrote them. Since *Myōjō* was a monthly magazine he was immediately able to show off her ability to make his ideas work. He did this with several series of her tanka as well as in a "response and reply" feature where one author posted a tanka dedicated to someone in an issue and in the next issue was a poem in reply. In this way, the rapid-developing affair was a very public spectacle though only a very few people were actually in the know. This open-secret situation made both of the authors even more daring with their comments and poem subjects.

It is evident, through letters to Tekkan Yosano, that already in November of 1900, Akiko had plans for a book of her tanka, and that Tekkan had promised he would help her get it published.

However, when Akiko compiled the tanka in her book she seems to have shuffled the original order of the events and the resulting poems so the casual reader could not follow her history. Being ripped from their original context adds ambiguity and mystery to many of the poems. In no way is the book, *Midaregami – Tangled Hair*, a narrative of a love affair, or a reproduction of those longer poem series, but rather a selection from a greater number of tanka written from the time in August, 1900 to July, 1901. In that time she had written and published over 630 tanka of which she put 284 in the book. Also she included another 115 tanka which had never been published.

She opens the book with her identification – her right to say and write about the events and ideas to follow. She wisely picked some of her tanka with the most controversial subject matter to be placed in the beginning as well those that best exhibited her new grammar – her pervasive use of *no* – of, and the lines that were often strings of nouns with only one or two verbs in the whole poem. In spite of efforts by translators to make English sentences out of her tanka, Akiko was using sentence fragments and phrases to carry her ideas. Collectively the poems reveal, not a sweet girl in love, but an absolute magisterial goddess with, as Janine Beichman writes: "her body and soul appearing and disappearing in the midst of primordial chaos. "

In the July, 1901, issue of *Myōjō* Tekkan announced under Member News that "Hō Akiko had come to Tokyo to study" and proclaimed that *Midaregami* would be published on the 20th of July. It had been previously announced in the May issue of *Myōjō*. As with so many publications of poetry, the book did not appear until later – August 15, 1901 under the joint name of Tokyo Shinshisha (Tokyo New Poetry Society) and the publisher Itō Bunyūkan.

The slight volume, 3 ½ inches across and 7 ½ inches tall, with 138 pages cost 35 *sen* – or about 2,520 in today's yen. It contained 399 tanka with no more than 3 to a page. The cover and 7 full-color illustrations were done by Fujishima Takeji (1867-1943), of the White Horse Society – an avant-garde group of artists.

The design of the cover illustration combined the idea of tangled hair with the Jugendstil styled red hair swirling around the face of the woman in a green heart. Below the heart are three stylized blossoms of Japanese design and below them are the red drops of blood that spelled out the title.

As with any so radical book the critics were deeply divided. Persons interested in the new poetry in tanka were delighted to find someone who could break the strangle-hold of the current rules and methods of tanka writing – to let in new life and fresh air. Akiko was able to do with her writing what many believed needed changing, not only in tanka, but all literature in Japan.

In addition her subject matter – the most intimate images of sexuality and femininity – titillated the readers accustomed only to birds and flowers in tanka. Her flight into freedom opened up vistas of new tanka subject matter and vocabulary for herself and others. However, she was a rare and outstanding poetic talent so that her tanka remained highly praised and held far above any other tanka work for the rest of the century which she had opened with such vigor.

The book became so highly esteemed that even though Akiko continued to write and publish books all her long life, none were as popular as her first. In later years, she tried to revise many of the poems and even called them "trite" and "too ambiguous" but this did not affect the popularity of her first book and her status as the most popular tanka writer since Murasaki Shikibu was writing one thousand years ago.

There were critics, mostly leaders in the tanka scene, who gave the book negative reviews. Mokichi Saitō, leader of the Araragi school, called her tanka "the precocious prattle of a young girl." Many readers found the poems unintelligible and of course, far too sexy for publication – especially since they came from a woman. The book broke too many taboos about the place of females in life and in poetry, and what was proper for them to say or even think, in the refined atmosphere of tanka – that most elegant poetry form.

In addition, some of the reasons for the initial negative interest in *Midaregami* came from various scandals in which Tekkan was involved. In the autumn of 1900 Masaoke Shiki (1861-1903), the famous writer of the day, challenged Tekkan to a debate about the current situation of tanka. At first Tekkan accepted but then when his life became complicated with the on-going affairs with both Akiko and Tomiko, and the birth of his baby with his common-law wife Takino, he fell ill and canceled the meeting. The men around Shiki saw this as a weakness as result of his morals. A book, *Bundan Shōmu Kyō – Tell-Tale Mirror: A Portrait of a Demon of the Literary World* was published anonymously in Tokyo that clearly targeted Tekkan and his many affairs. Also, since the family of his previous wife was no longer supporting him, it was known that Tekkan was pawning his possessions to pay his bills. There were three months *Myōjō* did not appear because of a lack of funds.

At the time there was great debate in Tokyo about the use of female nudes in art and the White Horse Society, of which Takeji Fujishima was an active member, was naturally on the side of using nude images. His artwork in *Tangled Hair*, along with the language and images of Akiko's poetry, set the book in the center of this debate.

In November, 1900, the cover of Tekkan's magazine, *Myōjō,* had carried a drawing of a full length nude. The issue was confiscated by the government to be destroyed and the magazine shut down for a month which only added to the scandals.

Still writers in other genres also recognized Akiko's talents and her boldness which they aspired to copy in their romantic works. Her influence spread beyond tanka to raise the standards of all Japanese literature.

CAST OF CHARACTERS

Akiko Yosano was born on December 7th, 1878 in Sakai, near Osaka, and named Shō Hō (or Otori). Her prosperous merchant family ran a famous shop—it supplied the Imperial Household - where they made and sold *yokan*— a sweet bean paste wrapped in bamboo leaves. Two months before her birth the family's only son—born to her father's previous wife, died in an accident. Her father had hoped she would be the boy to replace him. When he found out the expected child was a girl, he left the family. Thus, for three years she was forced to live with an aunt until another son was born. Overcoming her father's hatred of her, she began working in the shop by the age of 11 and when she was still in school she took over the management of the confectionary shop until she left home at the age of 20. To avoid name changes, she is referred to as Akiko Yosano, throughout this book even though Akiko was her pen name and she married Tekkan Yosano two months after the publication of *Midaregami*. For most of her married life she was the one who supported the family with her prolific writing of poetry, translations and essays on feminism while bearing 13 children – 11 of which survived. She also founded a school, *Bunka Gakuin* – Institute of Culture, where she was first dean and chief lecturer. She died of a stroke at the age of 63 in 1942 and her grave is in the Tama Reien on the outskirts of Tokyo.

Masako Masuda (1880–1946) was a lover of Tekkan that he called White Plum Blossom. She remained his friend even after his marriage to Akiko. In spite of her jealousy, Akiko became her friend also and together they worked on an anthology of tanka, *Robe of Love*. She later married to become Masako Chino.

Sadako Asada (1870-1953) was the first of Tekkan's live-in girlfriends / wives. She came from a wealthy family, in Tokuyama. She bore Tekkan a daughter in the autumn of 1899 which died before the end of the year. Tekkan left her shortly afterwards.

Takino Hayashi (1878-1966) was the daughter of a wealthy landowner in Izumomura. She met Tekkan while he was a teacher at the girls' school she attended. They began living together in 1899. After she had a son in 1900, Tekkan tried to have her become his wife officially and to register the boy in the Yosano family but Takino's father refused to accept this action and began to pressure Takino to leave Tekkan. Her father had been supporting the couple so it was his money that allowed Tekkan to publish *Myōjō*. For this help Tekkan listed Takino on the masthead of the magazine but she had no interest in poetry. Her nickname between Akiko and Tekkan was *Fuyō* – Hibiscus.

Tekkan Yosano – Hiroshi (1873–1935) was the son of an impoverished priest of the Jōda Shinshu sect, who was also a tanka writer. He educated his son in Japanese and Chinese literature so that later Tekkan was able to teach these subjects in various girls' schools. At the age of sixteen Tekkan was ordained as a priest, but opted to teach instead of entering a temple. It was while at the Tokuyama Girls School that he began an affair with the first of two women who would bear his illegitimate children. After he left the school, Tekkan worked for the publisher Meiji Shoin where he got the idea of starting his own magazine, *Myōjō – Bright Star* or *Morning Star* in April, 1900, in newspaper format. He formed The New Poetry Society in order to propagate his theories on modern ways to write tanka and other forms of poetry. Akiko's nickname for him was White Plum.

Tomiko Yamakawa (1879–1909) was the daughter of a samurai family. Because her father was the local banker in Fukui Prefecture, Tomiko was able to go to a prestigious girls' school. While still a student she began publishing her tanka in various magazines and was one of the earliest contributors to Tekkan's *Myōjō*. Through this, and Tekkan, she met, and became friends with Akiko. It soon happened that both girls fell in love with Tekkan and he with both of them—a factor that made them even greater friends. It was only at her father's insistence that she withdrew from the love triangle to prepare to marry. With many tears and threats of suicide she married ex-diplomat Tomeshichirō Yamakawa in April, 1901. He already had tuberculosis and died the next year. Tomiko then returned to the New Poetry Society and worked again with Akiko on the anthology *Robe of Love.* Now Tomiko had become infected with tuberculosis so that she died before she was thirty.

TIME-LINE OF THE AFFAIR

1900

April Tekkan Yosano wrote a poem asking Akiko to send some poems for his new magazine. She sent 7 tanka to him.

May Tekkan published 6 of them in *Myōjō*.

August Tekkan did a series of poetry workshops in the Osaka area.

August 4 Tekkan met with Tomiko in the morning.

August 4 Tekkan met with Akiko in the afternoon.

August 5 Akiko and Tomiko together attended a talk and workshop by Tekkan in Osaka.

August 6 It was decided to take a break from meetings so six men and the two women took the train to Takashi Beach, near Sakai, where they walked along the shore, wrote a great deal of poetry, had dinner, and left about 8:30.

August 8 The same 8 persons met again at Takashi Beach for the day.

August 9 Tekkan and Akiko with Tomiko and Kyōan went alone to the Suminoe Shrine where they amused themselves writing poetry on lotus leaves.

August 12 Another party was held at Takashi Beach. Tekkan tells Akiko of his marital troubles.

August 15 Akiko admits to Tekkan of her love for him.

August 24 Tekkan returns to Tokyo where four days later he falls ill with a mysterious fevered illness that Tekkan blames on a curse set on him by Akiko.

September Akiko publishes 41 of her newest tanka which she felt were inspired by her love for Tekkan. Sixteen of them were in *Myōjō* and the rest in *Kansai Bungaku* edited by Kawai Suimei.

September 23 Takino, Tekkan's common-law wife, has his son – Atsamu. Akiko sends her a letter with a congratulatory tanka.

October Akiko publishes 57 tanka.

November 4 Akiko travels to Osaka to be with Tomiko.

November 5 – 7 Tekkan meets the two women and they travel to Kyoto. From there they make a trip to Eikandō to see the colored leaves on Mt. Awata. They stay in an inn named Tsujino where Tekkan has the main room and the two women sleep together in an antechamber. It is at this time Tomiko reveals her father's plans for her marriage and by the end of the visit she has withdrawn from her relationship with Tekkan.

1901

January 9 – 10 Akiko and Tekkan meet secretly at Mt. Awata on the eastern side of Kyoto. At this time they promise to marry.

February In this issue of *Kansai Bungaku,* Tekkan published three poems in which he professes his love of Akiko.

February 15 In a letter from Akiko to Tekkan she threatens suicide if he will not let her join him in Tokyo.

March 10 A book is published anonymously in Tokyo, *Bundan Shōmu Kyō – Tell-Tale Mirror: Portrait of a Demon of Literature,* which casts Tekkan's behavior with women in a very bad light. The book is quoted in other newspapers and magazines which causes members to leave his group and begins to affect magazine sales. Tekkan tries to sue one of the suspected authors but loses the suit.

March 15 Tekkan publishes his book, *Tekkanshi – Child Tekkan.*

March 15? Takino writes to Akiko telling her she will return to her family and leaves Tekkan to Akiko.

March 20 Akiko again writes to Tekkan begging him to let her come to Tokyo.

March 29 Members of The New Poetry Society write to Tekkan asking him to give up Akiko and straighten out his marital affairs.

March 30 Takino and baby leave Tekkan's house.

April Tekkan publishes his book *Murasaki – Lavender* in which he portrays himself as a lover.

April 15? Tekkan moves from Kōjimachi Rokuban Chō to Shibuyamura — then a suburb of Tokyo consisting of small farms.

May 3 Tekkan writes to Akiko at once inviting her to join him and at the time rejecting her.

May 7 or 8 Takino and baby return to Tekkan saying she wanted to stay 2 or 3 years in the city until their son was educated.

May — end of Tekkan writes to Akiko asking her to come in June.

May 29 Akiko writes a letter that she is coming to Tokyo.

May 30 Tekkan postpones her trip to Tokyo until June 3rd. He offers to meet her at Mt. Awata but then cancels the trip.

June 6 Takino and baby leave Tokyo to return to her family home in Yamaguchi Prefecture.

June 9 Akiko went to Kyoto where she stayed with her step-sister, Sato. Akiko told her she was going to Tokyo to get her book published.

June 10 Akiko was met by Tekkan at the Shinbashi Station.

June 16 Akiko, for the first time, attended a meeting of The New Poetry Society. Members later recalled her shyness and yet noted her determination.

July issue of *Myōjō* carried Akiko's tanka sequence "Golden Wings" in the first pages. It also announced that member "Hō Akiko had arrived in Tokyo." It also carried an announcement of her book, *Midaregami*, to be released on July 15.

July 15 Akiko had compiled all the poems for the book. She picked the title from a poem Tekkan had given her in which he called her "Lady of the restless mind / of the tangled hair."

August 15 *Midaregami* was released to the public. It was just one year since the couple had met.

October Akiko and Tekkan were married.

The Tanka
from *Midaregami*
by Akiko Yosano

ENJI-MURASAKI – LIPSTICK-RED LAVENDER

1

夜の帳にささめき尽きし星の今を下界の人の鬢のほつれよ

yo no chō ni
sasameki tsukishi
hoshi no ima wo
gekai no hito no
bin no hotsure yo

bedroom curtains
the lovers' talk ends
now a star
one person of this earth
has stray hairs at the temple

2

歌にきけな誰れ野の花に紅き否むおもむきあるかな春罪もつ子

uta ni kike na
dare no no hana ni
akaki inamu
omomuki aru kana
haru tsumi motsu ko

ask among poems
who denies a bright red
to field flowers
a girl is also attractive
with her sin of scarlet

From the series "Scarlet Strings" which is considered as Akiko's manifesto
of her love for Tekkan.
Myōjō, May, 1901.

3

髪五尺ときなば水にやはらかき少女（おとめ）ごころは秘めて放たじ

kami goshaku
tokinaba mizu ni
yawarakaki
otome gokoro wa
himete hanataji

hair five feet
long loosened in water
softly sways
as does a young girl's heart
unable to free itself

4

血ぞもゆるかさむひと夜の夢のやど春を行く人神おとしめな

chi zo moyuru
kasan hitoyo no
yume no yado
haru wo yuku hito
kami otoshime na

blood burning
will lend to one's night
a lodging for dreams
for one passing in spring
the gods will not scorn

Myōjō, May 1901.

28

5

椿それも梅もさなりき白かりきわが罪問はぬ色桃に見る

tsubaki sore mo
ume mo sanariki
shirokariki
waga tsumi towanu
iro momo ni miru

pure white camellias
the same as *ume* plums that
do not allow my love
what never blames my sin
is only the color of peach

6

その子二十
櫛にながるる黒髪のおごりの春のうつくしきかな

sono ko hatachi
kushi ni nagaruru
kurokami no
ogori no haru no
utsukushiki kana

the girl is twenty
her hair is a black stream
running through a comb
in spring even pride
is beautiful

Shōtenchi, August, 1901.

7

堂の鐘のひくきゆふべを前髪の桃のつぼみに経たまへきみ

dō no kane no
hikuki yūbe wo
maegami no
momo no tsubomi ni
kyō tamae kimi

                     a temple bell
             softly rings at evening
                  my front hair
          adorned with a peach bud
        dear, chant your sutra for that

8

紫にもみうらにほふみだればこをかくしわづらふ宵の春の神

murasaki ni
momiura niou
midarebako wo
kakushi wazurau
yoi no haru no kami

               the scent of purple
          lingers on the red lining
             in a clothes basket;
              hiding it is hard
         for god in the spring evening

Myōjō, March, 1901.

9

臙脂色は誰にかたらむ血のゆらぎ春のおもひのさかりの命

enjiiro wa
dare ni kataran
chi no yuragi
haru no omoi no
sakari no inochi

dark red
to whom can I tell
the flaring blood
in a spring of passion
in the prime of life

10

紫の 濃き虹説きしさかづきに映る春の子眉毛かぼそき

murasaki no
koki niji tokishi
sakazuki ni
utsuru haru no ko
mayuge kabosoki

deep purple
he tells of rainbow love
over a wine cup
reflecting a girl in spring
with the thin eyebrows

11

紺青を絹にわが泣く春の暮れやまぶきがさね友歌ねびぬ

konjō wo
kinu ni waga naku
haru no kure
yamabukigasane
tomo uta nebinu

my weeping
the lining of cold blue silk
a spring sunset
in a multicolored yellow gown
my friend's tanka matures

12

まゐる酒に灯あかき宵を歌たまへ女はらから牡丹に名なき

mairu sake ni
hi akaki yoi wo
uta tamae
onna harakara
botan ni na naki

wine brings
the red light of evening
a poem
for a sisterhood
of unknown peonies

Myōjō, July, 1901.

13

海棠にえうなくときし紅捨てて夕雨みやる瞳よたゆき

kaidō ni
yōnaku tokishi
beni sutete
yūsame miyaru
hitomi yo tayuki

  a crab-apple tree
  with no need for rouge
  cast out
  looking at the evening rain
  these eyes are so weary

Myōjō, December, 1900.

14

水にねし嵯峨の大堰のひと夜神絽蚊帳の裾の歌ひめたまえ

mizu ni neshi
Saga no Õi no
hitoyogami
rogaya no suso no
uta hime tamae

  slept by the water
  of the Oi River at Saga
  a one-night god
  in the hem of the netting
  please keep our poem secret

The Oi River at Saga outside of Kyoto is ranked #10 of 382 attractions in
Kyoto.

15

春の国 恋の御国のあさぼらけしるきは髪か梅花のあぶら

haru no kuni
koi no mikuni no
asaborake
shiruki wa kami ka
baika no abura

spring country
blessed land of love
at daybreak
isn't my hair eye-catching
smelling of plum flowers

16

今はゆかむさらばと云ひし夜の神の御裾さはりてわが髪ぬれぬ

ima wa yukan
saraba to iishi
yo no kami no
misuso sawarite
waga kami nurenu

better go now
Good-bye says night god
as I toy
with his robe's hem
my hair gets wet

17
細きわがうなじにあまる御手のべてささへたまへな帰る夜の神

hosoki waga
unaji ni amaru
mite nobete
sasae tamae-na
kaeru yo no kami

the nape of my neck
is too small for your hand
held out
for support and plea
don't leave night god

18
清水へ祇園をよぎる桜月夜こよひ逢ふ人みなうつくしき

kiyomizu e
Gion wo yogiru
sakura zukiyo
koyoi ō hito
mina utsukushiki

at Kiyomizu Temple
going across Gion to see
moonlit cherry trees
this evening everyone
looks beautiful

The Kiyomizu Temple, one of the famous sites of Kyōto, was constructed without using a single nail. The veranda outside the main hall provides a wonderful view of the city. The unique atmosphere of Gion is particularly strong along Hanami-kōji Street and the Shirakawa River.

19

秋の神の御衣より曳く白き虹ものおもふ子の額に消えぬ

aki no kami no
mikeshi yori hiku
shiroki niji
mono omou ko no
hitai ni kienu

the god of autumn
trailing from his sacred clothes
a white rainbow
has vanished into the brow
of the young woman in love

20

経はにがし春のゆふべを奥の院の25菩薩歌うけたまへ

kyō wa nigashi
haru no yūbe wo
oku-no-in no
25 (nijū go) bosatsu
uta uketamae

a sutra is bitter
on a spring evening
where 25 saints
await the paradise bound
please accept my poem

Myōjō, March, 1901.

21

山ごもりかくてあれなのみをしへよ紅つくるころ桃の花さかむ

yamagomori
kakute are na no
mioshie yo
beni tsukuru koro
momo no hana sakan

stay secluded
that is your farewell
and teaching
my rouge will run out
just as peach trees bloom

Early in March, 1901, just before she married in April, Tomiko wrote a letter to Tekkan giving him to Akiko. This increased Akiko's desire to go to Tokyo to be with him, but he put her off as Takino, his common-law wife, and baby, were putting off the return to her family.

22

とき髪に
室むつまじの百合のかをり消えをあやぶむ夜の淡紅色よ

toki-gami ni
muro mutsumajino
yuri no kaori
kie wo ayabumu
yo no toki iro yo

my hair undone
in the room of love
a scent of lilies
I fear to lose
the pink of night

23

雲ぞ青き来し夏姫が朝の髪うつくしいかな水に流るる

kumo zo aoki
kishi natsuhime ga
asa no kami
utsukushii kana
mizu ni nagaruru

clouds so blue
the summer princess is here
how beautiful
her morning hair is
flowing in water

24

夜の神の朝のり帰る羊とらへちさき枕のしたにかくさむ

yo no kami no
asanori kaeru
hitsuji torae
chisaki makura no
shita ni kakusan

the night god
leaves in the morning
on a sheep
I'll catch and hide it
under a small pillow

25
みぎはくる牛かひ男歌あれな秋のみづうみあまりさびしき

migiwa kuru
ushikai otoko
uta are na
aki no mizuumi
amari sabishiki

coming by the shore
please herdsman sing
a song
the lake in autumn
is much too lonely

26.
やは肌のあつき血汐にふれも見でさびしからずや道を説く君

yawahada no
atsuki chishio ni
fure momide
sabishikarazu ya
michi wo toku kimi

soft skin
warm with heated blood
not touching it
on the path of virtue
aren't you lonely?

Akiko thought it was Tekkan's feelings of morality, he had been trained to
be a priest – his family's occupation, that kept him from her. She evidently
did not know it was his attachment to his common-law wife, Takino
Hayashi, who was awaiting the birth of their child.
Myōjō, October, 1900.

27
許したまへあらずばこその今のわが身うすむらさきの酒うつ
くしき

yurushi tamae
arazu ba kosono
ima no waga mi
usumurasaki no
sake utsukushiki

forgive this bad one
who shouldn't even be here
like me
pale purple wine
is so beautiful

28
わすれがたきとのみに趣味をみとめませ説かじ紫その秋の花

wasure gataki
tonomini shumi wo
mitome mase
tokaji murasaki
sono aki no hana

hard to forget
the one whose tastes
you should accept
leave the gromwell alone
with its purple autumn flower

Lithospermum - gromwell or stoneseed is a low-growing shrub of the
borage herb family. The small, glossy white nut-like seeds appear after the
deep purple flowers.

29
人かへさず暮れむの春の宵ごこち小琴にもたす乱れ乱れ髪

hito kaesazu
kuren no haru no
yoi gokochi
ogoto ni motasu
midare midaregami

> keeping you here
> in the twilight of spring
> almost drunk
> leaning on a small harp
> my tangled hair tangles

The *koto* is the national instrument of Japan. Koto is about 71 inches in length, and made from *kiri* wood. They have 13 strings that are strung over 13 movable bridges. Players adjust the string pitches by moving these bridges. They use three finger picks - on thumb, index finger, and middle finger - to pluck the strings.

30
たまくらに鬢のひとすぢきれし音を小琴と聞きし春の夜の夢

tamakura ni
bin no hitosuji
kireshi ne wo
ogoto to kikishi
haru no yo no yume

> pillowed on your arm
> a hair from my temple
> snapped
> the sound of a harp
> in a spring night's dream

31

春雨にぬれて君こし草の門よおもはれ顔の海棠の夕

harusame ni
nurete kimi koshi
kusa no kado yo
omoware gao no
kaidō no yū

in spring rain
dripping you came to
my little house
a crab apple flower
beloved girl in twilight

Myōjō, July, 1901.

32

小草いひぬ「酔へる涙の色にさかむそれまで斯くて覚めざれな少女」

ogusa iinu
"yoeru namida no
iro ni sakan
soremade kakute
samezarena otome"

the grass said
tears of rapture will bloom
into colors
until then, stay as you are
don't wake up dear girl

Myōjō, March, 1901.

33

牧場いでて南にはしる水ながしさても緑の野にふさふ君

makiba idete
minami ni hashiru
mizu nagashi
sate mo midori no
no ni fusau kimi

> from the meadow
> water runs a long way
> to the south
> how perfectly they match
> my lover and green fields

34

春よ老いな藤によりたる夜の舞殿ゐならぶ子らよ束の間老い
な

haru yo oina
fuji ni yoritaru
yo no maidono
inarabu kora yo
tsuka no ma oina

> spring don't grow old
> wisteria close to the night
> dancing stage
> in a row are the children
> momentarily older than this

Wistera is a member of the legume family native to Japan and China. The vines can grow up to ten feet in a year as they curl around supports. The pendulous racemes, 1 to 3 feet long, are either purple, lavender, or white. *Wisteria Maiden* is a Japanese subject for folk painting thought to have been inspired by popular kabuki dances of the same name. These paintings were often sold as good-luck charms for marriages.

35

雨みゆるうき葉しら蓮絵師の君に傘まゐらする三尺の船

ame miyuru
ukiha shira hasu
eshi no kimi ni
kasa mairasuru
sanjaku no fune

seeing raindrops
slip on white lotus leaves
my lover paints
under the umbrella offered
by a silly woman in a boat

The white lotus is not a water lily but of the family *Nelumbo nucifera*. The roots are planted in the soil of the pond or river bottom, while the leaves float on top of the water surface. The flowers are usually found on thick stems rising several centimeters above the leaves. The leaves may be as large as 2 feet in diameter, while the showy flowers can be over a foot in diameter.

36

御相いとどしたしみやすきなつかしき若葉木立の中の廬舎那仏

misō itodo
shitashimi yasuki
natsukashiki
wakaba kodachi no
naka no Rushanabutsu

a sacred face
is so easy to love
unforgettable
among the leaves on a hill
a famous Buddha image

In the Eastern Great Temple of the Buddhist temple complex located in the city of Nara is the Great Buddha Hall that houses the world's largest bronze statue of the Buddha also known in Japanese as *Daibutsu*.

37
さて責むな高きにのぼり君みずや紅の涙の永劫のあと

sate semuna
takaki ni nobori
kimi mizu ya
ake no namida no
yōgō no ato

don't blame me
from the hilltop castle
can't you see
the eternal trace
of my red tears

38
春雨にゆふべの宮をまよひ出でし子羊きみをのろはしの我れ

harusame ni
yūbe no miya wo
mayoi ideshi
kohitsuji kimi wo
norowashi no ware

in spring rain
last night from the palace
wandered
you the lamb
I want to curse

39

ゆあみする泉の底の小百合花二十の夏をうつくしと見ぬ

yuami suru
izumi no soko no
sayuri bana
hatachi no natsu o
utsukushi to minu

taking a bath
at the bottom of a spring
a lily flower
of twenty summers
looks beautiful

Tekkan's nickname for Tomiko was "White Lily."

40

みだれごこちまどひごこちぞ頻なる百合ふむ神に乳おほひあ
へず

midare gokochi
mayoi-gokochi zo
shikiri naru
yuri fumu kami ni
chichi ōi aezu

tangled feelings
among puzzled feelings
so often
the god tramples on the lily
bare breasts can't be covered

41

くれなゐの薔薇のかさねの唇に霊の香のなき歌のせますな

kurenai no
bara no kasane no
kuchibiru ni
rei no ka no naki
uta nosemasuna

the red
of the rose layered
on my lips
give me a poem
with soul fragrance

42

旅のやど水に端居の僧の君をいみじと泣きぬ夏の夜の月

tabi no yado
mizu ni hashii no
sō no kimi wo
imiji to nakinu
natsu no yo no tsuki

the travelers' inn
cooling off by the water
you a priest
so cruel the moon weeps
on a summer night

43

春の夜の闇の中くるあまき風しばしかの子が髪に吹かざれ

haru no yo no
yami no naka kuru
amaki kaze
shibashi kano ko ga
kami ni fukazare

at night in spring
coming through the darkness
a sweet breeze
don't blow for a while
this hair of a girl

44

水に飢ゑて森をさまよふ子羊のそのまなざしに似たらずや君

mizu ni uete
mori wo samayou
kohitsuji no
sono manazashi ni
nitarazuya kimi

so thirsty
wandering in the forest
a lamb
its eyes resemble yours
don't they

45

誰ぞ夕ひがし生駒の山の上のまよひの雲にこの子うらなへ

dare zo yūbe
higashi Ikoma no
yama no ue no
mayoi no kumo ni
kono ko uranae

who on this evening
looking east to Mt.Ikoma
above the peak
could tell fortunes with
a stray cloud for me

Mount Ikoma, over 2000 ft. high, was an important object of worship. On the east foot of the mountain, the 'Shrine for Mount Ikoma,' has been extant since the 5th century.

46

悔いますなおさへし袖に折れし剣つひの理想の花に刺あらじ

kuimasuna
osaeshi sode ni
oreshi tsurugi
tsui no omoi no
hana ni toge araji

do not regret
the sleeve stopped
and broke the sword
our ultimate ideal is
a flower without thorns

47

額ごしに暁の月みる賀茂川の浅水色のみだれ藻染よ

nuka goshi ni
ake no tsuki miru
Kamogawa no
asamizuiro no
midare mozome yo

over my brow
is the moon at daybreak
in Kamo River
the cloth is dyed light blue
with tangled waterweed

The banks of Kamogawa = Duck River are popular walking spots for
residents and tourists. The river is fairly shallow which accounts for the
growth of waterweeds. In some places the river is so low one can cross on
stepping stones or just get the hem of a kimono wet.

48

御袖くくりかへりますかの薄闇の欄干夏の賀茂川の神

misode kukuri
kaeri masuka no
usuyami no
obashima natsu no
Kamogawa no kami

in summer twilight
tucking up his sleeves
shall we go
said the god of Kamo River
at the railing of a bridge

49
なほ許せ御国遠くば夜の御神紅盃船に送りまゐらせむ

nao yuruse
mikuni tōkuba
yo no mikami
benisarafune ni
okuri mairasen

pardon me and
if your sacred land is far
god of night
I will offer as send-off
a boat as a red wine cup

50
狂ひの子我に焔の翅かろき百三十里あわただしの旅

kurui no ko
ware ni honō no
hane karoki
hyaku sanjū ri
awatadashi no tabi

a child of madness
my feathers of flame
are light to fly
a hundred thirty leagues
a journey of haste

This tanka describes Akiko's journey from Osako to Tokyo. Akiko's
reception in Tokyo was so unwelcoming that she evidently felt she had
been too hasty to come.
Myōjō, July, 1901.

51

今ここにかへりみすればわがなさけ闇をおそれぬめしひに似たり

ima koko ni
kaerimi sureba
waga nasake
yami wo osorenu
meshii ni nitari

now here
I find looking back
my passion
like a blind one who
never fears darkness

When Akiko and Tekkan met on August 15, 1900, this was her reply to
Tekkan's phrase, "I'll not forget" in an exchange of poems.

52

うつくしき命を惜しと神のいひぬ願ひのそれは果たしてし今

utsukushiki
inochi wo oshi to
kami no iinu
negai no sorewa
hatashiteshi ima

a beautiful life
too good to lose
said my god
now when
that wish was fulfilled

53

わかき小指 胡粉をとくにまどひあり夕ぐれ寒き木蓮の花

wakaki oyubi
gofun wo toku ni
madoi ari
yūgure samuki
mokuren no hana

young little finger
the pigment dissolves
with a waver
evening air chills
a magnolia flower

Rouge was used as lipstick. It was applied by licking the little finger, scooping up a bit of color from the ceramic jar to rub on the lips.

54

ゆるされし朝よそほひのしばらくを君に歌へな山の鶯

yurusareshi
asa yosooi no
shibaraku wo
kimi ni utaena
yama no uguisu

allowed
in the morning to get dressed
for awhile
please sing for him
mountain bush warbler

The Japanese bush warbler – *Cettia diphone*, is a bird more often heard than seen. Its distinctive breeding call can be heard throughout much of Japan from the start of spring. The beauty of its song is why it is sometimes called the Japanese nightengale.

55

ふしませとその間さがりし春の宵衣桁にかけし御袖かつぎぬ

fushimase to
sono ma sagarishi
haru no yoi
ikō ni kakeshi
misode katsuginu

good night
I left the room
in spring dusk
touching the sleeve of
your clothes on a hanger

56

みだれ髪を京の島田にかへし朝ふしてゐませの君ゆりおこす

midaregami wo
kyō no shimada ni
kaeshi asa
fushite imase no
kimi yuriokosu

tangled hair
changed to the unmarried style
in the morning
as you lie asleep
I try to wake you

Kyō no shimada is one of the various styles of piling the hair on top of the head in an elongated chignon. At that time, only young girls wore the style.

57
しのび足に君を追ひゆく薄月夜右のたもとの文がらおもき

shinobiashi ni
kimi wo oiyuku
usu-zukiyo
migi no tamoto no
fumigara omoki

    tip-toeing
  to follow you in the dim
    moonlight
  my right sleeve heavy
with letters now useless

58
紫に小草が上へ影おちぬ野の春かぜに髪けづる朝

murasaki ni
ogusa ga ue e
kage ochinu
no no haru kaze ni
kami kezuru asa

    the purple
  of a shadow was cast
    on low grasses
  spring winds of the field
comb it in the morning

59

絵日傘をかなたの岸の草になげわたる小川よ春の水ぬるき

ehigasa wo
kanatano kishi no
kusa ni nage
wataru ogawa yo
haru no mizu nuruki

tossed in the grass
a picture parasol on
the other shore
wading across the stream
the spring water is so warm

60

白壁へ歌ひとつ染めむねがひにて笠はあらざりき二百里の旅

shira kabe e
uta hitotsu some'n
negai nite
kasa wa arazariki
nihyaku ri no tabi

writing a poem
on a white wall is
my one desire
is to have no travel hat
for a 200 league journey

61

嵯峨の君を歌に仮せなの朝のすさびすねし鏡のわが夏姿

Saga no kimi wo
uta ni kasena no
asa no susabi
suneshi kagami no
waga natsu sugata

in Saga you left me
to join in poem making
morning solace
is finding in my mirror
a sulky woman in summer

Saga is the capital of the Saga prefecture in the northwest part of the island of Kyushu which touches both the Sea of Japan and the Ariake Sea.

62

ふさひ知らぬ新婦かざすしら萩に今宵の神のそと片笑みし

fusai shiranu
niibito kazasu
shirahagi ni
koyoi no kami no
soto kataemishi

unbalanced
the bride hides her face
in white bush clover
tonight's god
has a half-smile

Lespedeza is a genus of flowering plants in the pea family, commonly known as bush clovers or Japanese clovers. These shrubby plants or trailing vines are native to warm temperate to subtropical regions.

63

ひと枝の野の梅をらば足りぬべしこれかりそめのかりそめの別れ

hitoeda no
no no ume oraba
tarinu beshi
kore karisome no
karisome no wakare

taking a branch
from the wild apricot
is surely enough
this is only temporary
only a temporary parting

Ume – a variety of early blooming apricot has been wrongly translated as "plum" in Japanese poetry for so long it is hard to change it to a more accurate term.
This tanka was written in reply to Tekkan's "I cannot decide / is this brief?/ I cannot decide/ is this forever? / Will I always remember?" Akiko repeats the term "brief" but uses it to describe a parting, not the affair as Tekkan meant it.
Myōjō, May, 1901.

64

鶯は君が夢よともどきながら緑のとばりそとかかげ見る

uguisu wa
kimi ga yume yo to
modoki nagara
midori no tobari
soto kakage miru

that bush warbler
was only in your dream
at the same time
raising the green curtain
I quietly look outside

This tanka was in reply to Tekkan's new style poem in four parts: "yama no yu no ke kunjite / obashima ni tsubaki otsuru / tobari age yo / zuko zo uguisu no koe – the mountain's steam from hot water smells sweet / on the railing camellias are falling / raise the veil / from where does it came / the voice of the bush warbler" *Myōjō,* May 1901.

65

紫の虹の滴り花におちて成りしかひなの夢うたがふな

murasaki no
niji no shitatari
hana ni ochite
narishi kainano
yume utagauna

purple trickles
from the rainbow to drop
on a flower
dreams do come true
I have not doubt

Myōjō, July, 1901.

66

ほととぎす嵯峨へは一里京へ三里水の清瀧 夜の明けやすき

hototogisu
Saga e wa 1-ri
Kyō e 3-ri
mizu no Kiyotaki
yo no akeyasuki

the cuckoo
flies 1 league to Saga
3 leagues to Kyoto
to the waters of Kiyotaki
dawn comes quickly

Hototogisu – Lesser Cuckoo – *Cuculus poliocephalus* a bird native to Japan.
Kiyotaki is a small village on the west side of Kyōto. The Kiyotaki River
contains giant salamanders and the area is famous for walking and hiking.

67

紫の理想の雲はちぎれちぎれ仰ぐわが空それはた消えぬ

murasaki no
risō no kumo wa
chigire chigire
aogu waga sora
sore hata kienu

the purple
in the cloud of the ideal
is torn again
looking into my sky
it has vanished

68

乳ぶさおさへ神秘のとばりそとけりぬここなる花の紅ぞ濃き

chibusa osae
shinpi no tobari
soto kerinu
kokonaru hana no
kurenai zo koki

covering my breasts
the veil of secrets softly
kicked aside
here the flower's red
is deep and very dark

This was the first stanza from the series "Fallen Camellias."
Myōjō, March, 1901.

69

神の背にひろきながめをねがはずや今かたかたの袖こむらさき

kami no sena ni
hiroki nagame wo
negawazuya
ima katakata no
sode komurasaki

why not pray
to the back of god
for a wide view
then my sleeve will have
a dark purple mate

70

とや心朝の小琴の四つの緒のひとつを永久に神きりすてし

toya kokoro
asa no ogoto no
yotsu no o no
hitotsu wo towani
kami kirisuteshi

so my heart
this morning the small harp
with four strings
one of which has been taken
away forever by the god

71

ひく袖に片笑もらす春ぞわかき朝のうしほの恋のたはぶれ

hiku sode ni
kataemi morasu
haru zo wakaki
asa no ushio no
koi no tawabure

tugging a sleeve
to uncover a half-smile
in spring the youngster
on a tide of morning
plays at love

72

くれの春隣すむ絵師うつくしき今朝山吹に声わかかりし

kure no haru
tonari sumu eshi
utsukushiki
kesa yamabuki ni
koe wakakarishi

end of spring
next-door lives a painter
beautiful
this morning over roses
his voice seems young

Yamabuki – mountain breath – *Kerria Japonica* is also called a yellow rose,
because it is in the rose family, but the flowers are only about 1 inch across
and grow on racemes more like spirea.
Myōjō, July, 1901.

73

郷人にとなり邸のしら藤の花はとのみに問ひもかねたる

satobito ni
tonari yashiki no
sirafuji no
hana wa to nomini
toi mo kanetaru

my countryman
next door at the villa
of white wisteria
I ask about the flowers
but hesitate to say more

74

人にそひて樒ささぐるこもり妻母なる君を御墓に泣きぬ

hito ni soite
shikimi sasaguru
komorizuma
haha naru kimi wo
mihaka ni nakinu

along with you
as common law wife
I offer the anise
to your mother in the tomb
in tears

Shikimi – the latin name *Skimmia,* is taken from the Japanese. This evergreen plant is very pungent and often called wild anise. The leaves and flowers are used as offerings at grave sites because they stay green after being cut. During the tyrst of January 6 – 11, 1901, the union between Akiko and Tekkan was consumated and they began to talk of marrage.

75

なにとなく君に待たるるここちして出でし花野の夕月夜かな

nanitonaku
kimi ni mataruru
kokochi shite
ideshi hana no no
yūzukiyo kana

a vague feeling
you are waiting for me
I go out
in a flowering field
on a moonlit evening

This was considered the best tanka from the series in the September issue
of *Myōjō*. In later years Akiko still liked this tanka. Most of them in the
book she confessed to not liking and many she revised in later editions.
Myōjō, September, 1900.

76

おばしまにおもひはてなき身をもたせ小萩をわたる秋の風見る

obashima ni
omoi hatenaki
mi o motase
kohagi o wataru
aki no kaze miru

against the handrail
with endless thoughts
my body leans
to embrace the bush clover
the autumn wind

Myōjō, October, 1900.

77

ゆあみして泉を出でしわがはだにふるるはつらき人の世のきぬ

yuami shite
izumi o ideshi
waga hada ni
fururu wa tsuraki
hito no yo no kinu

after my bath
at the hot spring
these clothes
as rough to my skin
as the world

Myōjō, October, 1900.

78

売りし琴にむつびの曲をのせしひびき逢魔がどきの黒百合折れぬ

urishi koto ni
mutsubi no kyoku wo
noseshi hibiki
ōmagadoki no
kuroyuri orenu

the harp sold
the music in perfect union
layers the sound
of twilight when a black lily
snaps

The black lily is part of several Japanese legends of jealousy.

79

うすものの二尺のたもとすべりおちて蛍ながるる夜風の青き

usumono no
nishaku no tamoto
suberi ochite
hotaru nagaruru
yokaze no aoki

from the gauze
of the two foot kimono sleeve
the slip
of a firefly drifting
in blue evening wind

80

恋ならぬねざめたたずむ野のひろさ名なし小川のうつくしき夏

koi naranu
nezame tatazumu
no no hirosa
na nashi ogawa no
utsukushiki natsu

aching with love
unable to sleep I stand
before a wide field
even an unnamed brook
is beautiful in summer

81

このおもひ何とならむのまどひもちしその昨日すらさびしかりし我れ

kono omoi
nani to naran no
madoi mochishi
sono kinō sura
sabishikarishi ware

> this feeling of love
> comes and goes
> I doubted it
> even yesterday when
> it made me lonely

82

おりたちてうつつなき身の牡丹見ぬそぞろや夜を蝶のねにこし

oritachite
utsutsu naki mi no
botan miyu
sozoro ya yoru wo
chō no ne ni koshi

> so distraught
> as if in a dream I saw
> a peony
> suddenly in the night
> a butterfly comes to sleep

Botan – peony The peony is named after Paeon, also spelled Paean, a student of Asclepius, the Greek god of medicine and healing. When Asclepius became jealous of his pupil; Zeus saved Paeon from his wrath by turning him into the peony flower.

83

その涙のごふゑにしは持たざりきさびしの水に見し二十日月

sono namida
nogou enishi wa
motazariki
sabishi no mizu ni
mishi hatsuka zuki

these tears
I did not have a chance
to wipe them
so lonely by the water
a late-rising moon

84

水十里ゆふべの船をあだにやりて柳による子ぬかうつくしき

mizu jūri
yūbe no fune wo
ada ni yarite
yanagi ni yoru ko
nuka utsukushiki

10 leagues of water
a boat in the evening
leaves me
leaning against the willow
a girl fragile and beautiful

85

旅の身の大河ひとつまどはむや徐 かに日記 の里の名けしぬ

tabi no mi no
ōkawa hitotsu
madowan ya
shizukani niki no
sato no na keshinu

            a traveler
        may lose her way
         at a large river
      slowly erasing the name
    of one's hometown in a diary

86

小傘 とりて朝の水くみ我とこそ穂麦 あをあを小雨ふる里

ogasa torite
asa no mizukumi
ware to koso
homugi aoao
kosame furu sato

        under a tiny umbrella
      to draw the morning water
            for me alone
       wheat spikes are green as
     light rain falls on the village

Myōjō, July, 1901.

69

87

おとに立ちて小川をのぞく乳母が小窓小雨のなかに山吹のちる

oto ni tachite
ogawa wo nozoku
uba ga komado
kosame no nakani
yamabuki no chiru

hearing a noise
the nurse sees a stream
from a small window
in a light rain
yellow rose petals fall

88

恋か血か牡丹に尽きし春のおもひとのゐの宵のひとり歌なき

koi ka chi ka
botan ni tsukishi
haru no omoi
tonoi no yoi no
hitori uta naki

love or blood
a peony absorbs
my feeling of spring
alone in a night palace
I can make no poem

Myōjō July, 1901.

89

長き歌を牡丹にあれの宵の殿 妻となる身の我れぬけ出でし

nagaki uta wo
botan ni are no
yoi no otodo
tsuma to naru mi no
ware nukeideshi

a long poem
requested about a peony
in the night palace
to become a bride
I slipped out of it

The poems, numbered 88 and 89, were placed together in the magazine. It
was very rare for Akiko to put her poems in the book in the arrangement
in which they were first published.
Myōjō, July, 1901.

90

春三月柱 おかぬ琴に音たてぬふれしそぞろの宵の乱れ髪

haru mitsuki
ji okanu koto ni
oto tatenu
fureshi sozoro no
yoi no midaregami

a harp without a bridge
for three months in spring
makes a sound
my tangled hair touched it
on a restless evening

91

いづこまで君は帰るといふべ野にわが袖ひきぬ翅 ある童

izuko made
kimi wa kaeru to
yūbe no ni
waga sode hikinu
hane aru warawa

how far away
are you from your home
in the evening field
my sleeve was plucked
by a child with wings

It is thought that *hane aru warawa* – a child with wings referred to cupid.
Myōjō, December. 1900.

92

ゆふぐれの戸に倚り君がうたふ歌「うき里去りて往きて帰らじ」

yūgure no
to ni yori kimi ga
utau uta
uki sato sarite
yukite kaeraji

in the evening
leaning against the door
you sing a song
I like to leave the cruel world
and never come back

From Akiko's memories of the August, 1900, visit to Mt. Awata.
Myōjō, December, 1900.

93

さびしさに百二十里をそぞろ来ぬと云ふ人あらばあらば如何
ならむ

sabishisa ni
hyakunijū ri o
sozoro kinu to
yū hito araba
araba ika naran

> so lonely
> I've come 120 leagues
> eager
> for someone to say
> how happy I could be

Akiko reminding Tekkan she wanted to come to Tokyo to live with him.
Myōjō, December, 1900.

94

君が歌に袖かみし子を誰と知る浪速の宿は秋寒かりき

kimi ga uta ni
sode kamishi ko wo
tare to shiru
naniwa no yado wa
aki samukariki

> hearing your poem
> someone bit her sleeve
> do you know who
> it was at the Osaka inn
> in the chill of autumn

In August, 1900, Akiko and Tekkan met five times. It was during the time
they were at Mt. Awata they first revealed their love to each other.
Myōjō, December, 1900.

95

その日より魂にわかれし我むくろ美しと見ば人にとぶらへ

sono hi yori
tama ni wakareshi
ware mukuro
utsukushi to miba
hito ni toburae

since that day
my soul has been apart
from my body
if you see it as beautiful
have a funeral for me

96

今の我に歌のありやを問ひますな柱 なき繊弦 これ二十五弦

ima no ware ni
uta no ariya wo
toi masuna
ji naki hosoito
kore nijūgo gen

now is not the time
for me to make poems
don't ask
a harp without a bridge
is only 25 thin strings

A Japanese harp – koto- originally had 13 strings. In 1969 Nosaka Keiko
added strings to make a harp with 20 strings. In 1991 she added 5 more
strings. A 25-string harp provides thinner strings and makes deeper
sound. Yet Akiko Yosano published this poem in 1901.

97
神のさだめ命のひびき終 の我世琴に斧うつ音ききたまへ

kami no sadame
inochi no hibiki
tsui no wagayo
koto ni ono utsu
oto kikitamae

God's rule
is the sound of life
at the end of mine
listen to an ax being
smashed into a harp

98
人ふたり無才の二字を歌に笑みぬ恋二万年ながき短き

hito futari
busai no niji wo
uta ni eminu
koi niman-nen
nagaki mijikaki

two people
smile at the two letters
inadequate
for 20,000 years of love
the long and short of it

HASU NO HANAFUNE – LOTUS FLOWER BOAT

99
漕ぎかへる夕船おそき僧の君紅蓮や多きしら蓮や多き

kogi kaeru
yūbune osoki
sō no kimi
guren ya ooki
shira-hasu ya ooki

rowing home
the evening boat so slow
you my priest
among the many red lotus
just as many white ones

100
あづまやに水のおときく藤の夕はづしますなのひくき枕よ

azumaya ni
mizu no oto kiku
fuji no yū
hazushimasuna no
hikuki makura yo

in the summer house
we hear the sound of water
on a wisteria night
do not take away
this low pillow

101

御袖ならず御髪のたけときこえたり七尺いづれしら藤の花

misode narazu
migushi no take to
kikoetari
nanashaku izure
shirafuji no hana

> not her sleeve
> but her hair they say
> in any case
> seven feet is the length
> of the white wisteria

The pendulous racemens of wisteria flowers are 4 – 30 inches long. The vines can cover up to an acre.

102

夏花のすがたは細きくれなゐに真昼生きむの恋よこの子よ

natsuhana no
sugata wa hosoki
kurenai ni
mahiru ikin no
koi yo kono ko yo

> a summer flower's
> shape is a slender scarlet
> wanting to live at noon
> all this love
> this girl child

103
肩おちて経にゆらぎのそぞろ髪をとめ有心者春の雲こき

kata ochite
kyō ni yuragi no
sozorogami
otome ushinja
haru no kumo koki

sliding from the shoulder
then swaying over the sutras
unruly hair
for a girl who is sensitive
spring clouds are very dense

104
とき髪を若枝 にからむ風の西よ二尺に足らぬうつくしき虹

tokikami wo
wakae ni karamu
kaze no nishi yo
nishaku ni taranu
utsukushiki niji

unbound hair tangled
by wind on a green twig
flows to west
as a beautiful rainbow
less than 2 feet long

A correction in the book version. *Nishaku* was changed to *nishaku ni*.
Myōjō, September, 1901.

105

うながされて汀 の闇 に車おりぬほの紫の反橋 の藤

unagasarete
migiwa no yami ni
kuruma orinu
hono murasaki no
sorihashi no fuji

        enticed to
   the water's edge in darkness
     getting off the cart
  for wisteria's faint purple
    on the arched bridge

106

われとなく梭 の手とめし門 の唄姉がゑまひの底はづかしき

ware to naku
osa no te tomeshi
kado no uta
ane ga emai no
soko hazukashiki

     without realizing
   my hands stopped weaving
     a song at the gate
    when my sister smiled
    I blushed deep within

107
ゆあがりのみじまひなりて姿見に笑みし昨日の無きにしもあらず

yuagari no
mijimai narite
sugatami ni
emishi kinōno no
naki ni shimo arazu

after my bath
I dress myself smiling
in the long mirror
a portrait of yesterday
one cannot deny

108
人まへを袂すべりしきぬでまり知らずと云ひてかかへてにげぬ

hitomae wo
tamoto suberishi
kinudemari
shirazu to iite
kakaete nigenu

in front of people
a silk ball slipped
out of my sleeve
what is this, I said
holding it and ran away

109
ひとつ函
にひひなをさめて蓋とぢて何となき息桃にはばかる

hitotsu hako ni
hiina osamete
futa tojite
nani to naki iki
momo nihabakaru

laying in a box
the dolls of emperor and empress
and putting the lid on them
I hold back a sigh fearing
the peach blossoms hear it

Girls' Day is celebrated on the third day of the third month – now March 3. A stair-step display is covered with a red cloth to show off the doll collection of the family. Often dolls portraying the emperor and empress or famous persons are kept over generations. Peach trees bloom at this time so they are often part of the decorations or special foods.

110
ほの見しは奈良のはづれの若葉宿うすまゆずみのなつかしかりし

hono mishi wa
nara no hazure no
wakaba yado
usu mayu zumi no
natsukashikarishi

getting a glimpse
on the outskirts of Nara
at the inn of new leaves
someone with light eyebrows
is so dearly missed

111
紅に名の知らぬ花さく野の小道いそぎたまふな小傘の一人

ake ni na no
shiranu hana saku
no no komichi
isogitamauna
ogasa no hitori

red flowers bloom
their name unknown
on the field path
don't hurry the one
under a small umbrella

112
くだり船昨夜月かげに歌そめし御堂の壁も見えず見えずなり
ぬ

kudari bune
yobe tsuki kage ni
uta someshi
midoo no kabe mo
miezu miezu narinu

downstream a boat
last night in the moonlight
the poem I wrote
on the temple wall
fades and disappears

Memories of time spent with Tekkan in August.
Myōjō, December, 1900.

113
師の君の目を病みませる庵 の庭へうつしまゐらす白菊の花

shi no kimi no
me wo yamimaseru
io no niwa e
utsushi mairasu
shiragiku no hana

my master poet
suffers from eye trouble
in a garden hut
there I transplant flowers
my white chrysanthemum

Yellow or white chrysanthemum flowers of the species *C. morifolium* are boiled to make a sweet drink or applied as a compress to the eyes.

114
文字ほそく君が歌ひとつ染めつけぬ玉虫 ひめし小筥 の蓋 に

moji hosoku
kimi ga uta hitotsu
sometsukenu
tamamushi himeshi
kobako no futa ni

with thin letters
one of your poems
I wrote
on the lid of a small box
enshrining a jewel beetle

Tamamushi – jewel beetle – *Chrysochroa fulgidissima*, is a metallic colored woodboring beetle of the Buprestidae family that grows up to 1 ½ inches. Since this bug has iridescent wings that glow lengthwise with different colors depending upon the light angle, one cannot be sure exactly which color it is.

115

ゆふぐれを籠へ鳥よぶいもうとの爪先 ぬらす海棠の雨

yūgure wo
kago e tori yobu
imōto no
tsumasaki nurasu
kaidō no ame

in the evening
my sister calls birds
into the cage
rain wets her toes
by the crabapple tree

Kaidō is the flowering crabapple tree used for ornamental purposes.

116

ゆく春をえらびよしある絹袷衣
ねびのよそめを一人に問ひぬ

yuku haru wo
erabi yoshi aru
kinuawase
nebi no yosome wo
hitori ni toinu

late in spring
there are reasons to choose
a lined kimono
asking someone if
I look grown up

117

ぬしいはずとれなの筆の水の夕そよ墨足らぬ撫子がさね

nushi iwazu
torena no fude no
mizu no yū
soyo sumi taranu
nadeshiko gasane

it doesn't matter who
takes up a brush by the water
in the evening
yes, I am in lack of ink
in pink layered clothes

118

母よびてあかつき問ひし君といはれそむくる片頬柳にふれぬ

haha yobite
akatsuki toishi
kimi to iware
somukuru katahō
yanagi ni furenu

mother called me
to ask about you and
your dawn visits
as I turned away
the willow touched my cheek

119

のろひ歌かきかさねたる反古とりて黒き胡蝶をおさへぬるか
な

noroi uta
kaki kasanetaru
hogo torite
kuroki kochō wo
osae nurukana

cursing poems
as I write they pile up
in the trash
with waste paper I finally
catch a black butterfly

The only butterfly with completely black wings, on the topside, is the unlikely named Pink Rose - *Atrophaneura kotzebuea* - of the Papilionidae family

120

額しろき聖よ見ずや夕ぐれを海棠に立つ春夢見姿

nuka shiroki
hijiri yo mizuya
yūgure wo
kaidō ni tatsu
haru yumemi sugata

with a pale brow
dear saint don't you see
in the evening
a crab-apple tree where
a person dreams of spring

Myōjō, July, 1901.

121
笛の音に法華経うつす手をとどめひそめし眉よまだうらわかき

fue no ne ni
hokekyō utsusu
te wo todome
hisomeshi mayu yo
mada urawakaki

> at the flute's sound
> his hand stopped copying
> the sutra
> the eyebrows in a frown
> are still very young

Fue is the generic name for any native Japanese flute, often made of
bamboo with a breathy tone.
This is considered to be the result of Akiko's efforts to explore using tanka
to describe other people, other events, other than her own feelings.

122
白檀のけむりこなたへ絶えずあふるにくき扇をうばいぬるかな

byakudan no
kemuri konata e
taezu aoru
nikuki ōgi wo
ubainuru kana

> sandalwood smoke
> always being floated here
> blown by
> his damnable fan
> which I took away

Sandalwoods are medium-sized hemi-parasitic trees, and part of the same
botanical family as European mistletoe. Its woody fragrance makes it
prized for incense.
Poem was taken from a series written about the first meeting of Akiko and
Tekkan at Hamadera on the beach at Takashi on August 6, 1900.

123

母なるが枕経よむかたはらのちさき足をうつくしと見き

haha naru ga
makuragyō yomu
katawara no
chisaki ashi wo
utsukushi to miki

a mother
chants the death sutra
by the side
of such small feet
see how beautiful

Makuragyō – pillow sutra – a ceremony held as soon as possible after a
death that includes the burning of incense, a short reading from a sutra
and a short sermon. The face of the deceased is covered with a white cloth.
Another of Akiko's tanka experiments while observing others. It could
have come from Tekkan's story of his child born to Asada Sadako (1870-
1953) in October, 1899. The boy died before the end of the year.
Myōjō, October, 1900.

124

わが歌に瞳のいろをうるませしその君去りて十日たちにけり

waga uta ni
hitomi no iro wo
urumaseshi
sono kimi sarite
tooka tachinikeri

at my poem
the color of his eyes
is wet with tears
since you left
it's been ten days

After the five meetings of the lovers in August, 1900, Tekkan returned to
Tokyo and became ill. Thus he failed to write as he had promised.

125

かたみぞと風なつかしむ小扇のかなめあやふくなりにけるかな

katami zo to
kaze natsukashimu
ko-ōgi no
kaname ayauku
narinikeru kana

this keepsake
I loved so much the breeze
of a small fan
its pivot is nearly broken
from being used so much

There are two types of fans in Japan. The *ushiwa* is a rigid fan and the *ōgi* or *sensu* is a folding fan. Wooden staves are fastened at one end to form a pivot in order to spread out the paper or silk section for maximum air movement. As the group was leaving the inn at Takashi Beach in August, 1900, the maid brought in 8 fans. Each person autographed the fans and Tekkan wrote a few words under his name for Akiko.

126

春の川のりあひ舟のわかき子が昨夜の泊の唄ねたましき

haru no kawa
noriai bune no
wakaki ko ga
yobe no tomari no
uta netamashiki

on a spring river
a fellow passenger on the boat
is so very young
I am envious of his song
about last night's guest

127

泣かで急げやは手にはばき解くゑにしゑにし持つ子の夕を待たむ

nakade isoge
yawate ni
habaki toku enishi
enishi motsu ko no
yūbe wo mata'n

hurry up and don't cry
don't you think the one who is
untying your leggings
is so bound to you
she will wait until evening

Habaki / *kyahan*– leggings or gaiters.

128

燕なく朝をはばきの紐ぞゆるき柳かすむやその家のめぐり

tsubame naku
asa wo habaki no
himo zo yuruki
yanagi kasumu ya
sono ya no meguri

a swallow's song
this morning the string
of leggings loosened
the weeping willow a mist
around this very house

129
小川われ村のはづれの柳かげに消えぬ姿を泣く子朝見し

ogawa ware
mura no hazure no
yanagi kage ni
kienu sugata wo
naku ko asa mishi

       I was the stream
    at the end of the village
      in willow shade
  I saw a young maid weeping
for a man who vanished at dawn

130
鶯に朝寒からぬ京の山おち椿踏む人むつまじき

uguisu ni
asa samukaranu
kyō no yama
ochitsubaki fumu
hito mutsumajiki

     for a bush warbler
   mornings are not cold
     in Kyoto mountains
 the couple step in perfect union
   on the dropped camellia

Tanka taken from the series "Fallen Camellias."
Myōjō, May, 1901.

131

道たまたま蓮月が庵のあとに出でぬ梅に相行く西の京の山

michi tamatama
Rengetsu ga iori no
ato ni idenu
ume ni aiyuku
nishi no Kyō no yama

the road happened to lead us to
the relic hut of Sister Rengetsu
when we go to see
the apricot blossoms
on the mountains west of Kyoto

Rengetsu a woman poet (1791 – 1875) who lived in Kyoto. Her name was first Nobu, but after her husband passed away, she became a nun and changed her name.

132

君が前に李青蓮説くこの子ならずよき墨なきを梅にかこつな

kimi ga mae ni
Ri Seiren toku
kono ko narazu
yoki sumi naki wo
ume ni kakotsu na

in front of you
unable to praise a Chinese poet
this girl
is cannot to write a good poem
so don't blame apricot blossoms

李青蓮＝李白Libai = LiPo the famous Chinese poet

133

あるときはねたしと見たる友の髪に香の煙のはひかかるかな

aru toki wa
netashi to mitaru
tomo no kami ni
kō no kemuri no
hai kakaru kana

there were times
I looked with envy
at my friend's hair
the smoke of funeral
incense now trails over it

134

わが春の二十姿と打ぞ見ぬ底くれなゐのうす色牡丹

waga haru no
hatachi sugata to
uchi zo minu
soko kurenai no
usuiro botan

in the spring
of my twentieth year my figure
is at a glance
red-bottomed like
a pale pink peony

Myōjō, July, 1901.

135
春はただ盃にこそ注ぐべけれ智恵あり顔の木蓮や花

haru wa tada
sakazuki ni koso
tsugu bekere
chie ari gao no
mokuren ya hana

only in spring
should wisdom be poured
in a wine cup
here is the wise face
of a magnolia flower

136
さはいへど君が昨日の恋がたりひだり枕の切なき夜半よ

sa wa iedo
kimi ga kinō no
koigatari
hidari makura no
setsu naki yahan yo

though I said
I didn't care about your past
tales of love
sadness on the left-hand pillow
made me cry in the dead of night

From the series "Fallen Camellias."
Myōjō, March, 1901.

137
人そぞろ宵の羽織の肩うらへかきしは歌か芙蓉といふ文字

hito sozoro
yoi no haori no
kata ura e
kakishi wa uta ka
fuyō to yū moji

who was so excited
that evening he wrote
cotton rose
on the lining of a coat
could you call it a poem?

Fuyō – cotton rose – a member of the hibiscus family was a flower or the
nickname of Tekkan's live-in wife – Takino.
From the series "Fallen Camellias."
Myōjō, March, 1901.

138
琴の上に梅の実おつる宿の昼よちかき清水に歌ずする君

koto no ue ni
ume no mi otsuru
yado no hiru yo
chikaki shimizu ni
uta zusuru kimi

on the harp
an apricot fruit falls
at a noon inn
by the clear spring
you recite a poem

139

うたたねの君がかたへの旅づつみ恋の詩集の古きあたらしき

utatane no
kimi ga kataeno
tabi zutsumi
koi no shishū no
furuki atarashiki

taking a nap
you lie beside the packed
travel bag
a collection of love poems
both old and new

140

戸に倚りて菖蒲売る子がひたひ髪にかかる薄靄にほひある朝

to ni yorite
ayame uru ko ga
hitai gami ni
kakaru usu moya
nioi aru asa

selling irises
a girl leans against a door
over her forehead hair
hanging in the thin haze
is a scent in the morning

The connection is that both the girl's hair and the iris have a slight scent early in the morning.

141

五月雨もむかしに遠き山の庵通夜する人に卯の花いけぬ

samidare mo
mukashi ni tooki
yama no io
tsuya suru hito ni
unohana ikenu

summer rains
also ceased so long ago
in a mountain retreat
keeping a vigil for someone
by arranging white flowers

142

四十八寺そのひと寺の鐘なりぬ今し江の北雨雲ひくき

shijū hachi ji
sono hito tera no
kane narinu
imashi e no kita
amagumo hikuki

48 temples
in one of them
a bell tolls
just now north of the bay
a rain cloud hangs low

Hō-on Daishi, a Buddhist priest, started to build 48 temples in the 16th century in Okayama Prefecture, close to Kyushu.

143

人の子にかせしは罪かわがかひな白きは神になどゆづるべき

hito no ko ni
kaseshi wa tsumi ka
waga kaina
shiroki wa kami ni
nado yuzurubeki

is it sin
to let him rest on
my arm pillow?
its pale skin
is the gift of god

From a series of memories of their trip in autumn to Mt. Awata.
Myōjō, December, 1900.

144

ふりかへり許したまへの袖だたみ闇くる風に春ときめきぬ

furikaeri
yurushitamae no
sodedatami
yami kuru kaze ni
haru tokimekinu

glancing back
with apologies I hastily
fold your clothes
a breeze comes through darkness
that flutters my spring heart

145

夕ふるはなさけの雨よ旅の君ちか道とはで宿とりたまへ

yū furu wa
nasake no ame yo
tabi no kimi
chikamichi towade
yado toritamae

dusk falls
with the blessings of rain
don't go
or ask for a shortcut
just find some lodging

Myōjō, March, 1901.

146

巖をはなれ谿をくだりて躑躅をりて都の絵師と水に別れぬ

iwa wo hanare
tani wo kudarite
tsutsuji orite
miyako no eshi to
mizu ni wakarenu

a large rock
far from the valley rift
splitting up azalea
I leave the city painter
and the water too

147

春の日を恋に誰れ倚るしら壁ぞ憂きは旅の子藤たそがるる

haru no hi wo
koi ni dare yoru
shirakabe zo
uki wa tabi no ko
fuji tasogaruru

on a spring day
one in love leans against
a white wall
troubled is a traveler
as dusk falls on wisteria

148

油のあと嶋田のかたと今日知りし壁に李の花ちりかかる

abura no ato
shimada no kata to
kyō shirishi
kabe ni sumomo no
hana chirikakaru

a spot of oil
from a woman's chignon
today I know
how the plum blossom
on the wall will scatter

Shimada is the chignon hair style for young women.

149
うなじ手にひくきささやき藤の朝をよしなやこの子行くは旅の君

unaji te ni
hikuki sasayaki
fuji no asa wo
yoshinaya kono ko
yuku wa tabi no kimi

> a hand on my neck
> the soft whisper of
> morning wisteria
> this girl can't keep
> her beloved traveler

150
まどひなくて経ずする我と見たまふか下品の仏上品の仏

madoi nakute
kyō zusuru ware to
mitamō ka
gebon no hotoke
jō bon no hotoke

> without disbelief
> I recite the sutras
> so there can't be
> lower Buddhists
> higher Buddhists

Myōjō, March, 1901.

151

ながしつる四つの笹舟紅梅を載せしがことにおくれて往きぬ

nagashi tsuru
yotsu no sasabune
kōbai wo
noseshi ga kotoni
okurete yukinu

drifting along
four bamboo leaf boats
red flowers
are carried by the one
that follows behind

152

奥の室のうらめづらしき初声に血の気のぼりし面まだ若き

oku no ma no
uramezurashiki
ubugoe ni
chi no ke noborishi
omo mada wakaki

from an inner room
how unusual to hear
a baby's first cry
the blood rises
in a face still young

Tekkan's common-law wife, Takino, gave birth to a son on September 23, 1900.
Kansai Bungaku, November, 1900.

153
人の歌をくちずさみつつ夕よる柱つめたき秋の雨かな

hito no uta wo
kuchizusamitsutsu
yūbe yoru
hashira tsumetaki
aki no ame kana

his poem
being recited this evening
while leaning
against the cold pillar
along with autumn rain

154
小百合さく小草がなかに君まてば野末にほひて虹あらはれぬ

sayuri saku
ogusa ga naka ni
kimi mateba
nozue nioite
niji arawarenu

lilies bloom
among small grasses
waiting for you
at the edge of a fragrant field
appears a rainbow

155

かしこしといなみていひて我とこそその山坂を御手に倚らざりし

kashikoshi to
inamite iite
ware to koso
sono yamasaka wo
mite ni yorazarishi

graciously
I had to refuse
so that
I went up the mountain
without holding his hand

156

鳥辺野は御親の御墓あるところ清水坂に歌はなかりき

Toribeno wa
mioya no mihaka
aru tokoro
Kiyomiz uzaka ni
uta wa nakariki

Toribeno
grave site of your parents
this is a place
on the slope of Kiyomitzu
where I find no poems

The historical Toribeno referred to an old burial ground known since the
Heian period in the Higashiyama area near Mt. Amidagamine in Kyoto.
The present day Toribeno is an extensive graveyard near Kiyomizu-dera.

157

御親まつる墓のしら梅中に白く熊笹小笹たそがれそめぬ

mioya matsuru
haka no shiraume
naka ni shiroku
kumazasa ozasa
tasogaresomenu

at your parents'
grave plum blossoms
white among the
low and tall bamboo grass
begins to darken

158

男きよし載するに僧のうらわかき月にくらしの蓮の花船

otoko kiyoshi
nosuru ni sō no
urawakaki
tsuki nikurashino
hasu no hanafune

a graceful man
aboard is a priest
very young
the moon is horrid
over lotus flower boat

159
経にわかき僧のみこゑの片明り月の蓮船兄こぎかへる

kyō ni wakaki
sō no mikoe no
kata-akari
tsuki no hasufune
ani kogikaeru

voice of the priest
too young to recite sutras
in dim moon light
my older brother rows him
back in the lotus boat

160
うき葉きるとぬれし袂の紅のしづく蓮にそそぎてなさけ教へむ

ukiha kiru to
nureshi tamoto no
ake no shizuku
hasu ni sosogite
nasake oshien

as a floating leaf is cut
my sleeve gets soaked
red drops
pour on the lotus leaf
to teach it sympathy

161
こころみにわかき唇ふれて見れば冷ややかなるよしら蓮の露

kokoromi ni
wakaki kuchibiru
furete mireba
hiya yaka naru yo
shira hasu no tsuyu

                    testing
              these young lips try
                   touching
              how cold is the dew
              on the white lotus

162
明くる夜の河はばひろき嵯峨の欄きぬ水色の二人の夏よ

akuru yo no
kawahaba hiroki
Saga no ran
kinu mizuiro no
futari no natsu yo

                 at daybreak
           the wideness of the river
                on the railings
           at Saga the blue robes
              of two in summer

163

藻の花のしろきを摘むと山みづに文がら濡ぢぬうすものの袖

mo no hana no
shiroki wo tsumu to
yamamizu ni
fumigara hijinu
usumono no sode

duck weeds
picking the white flower
on mountain water
it steals the old letter
from a sheer sleeve

164

牛の子を木かげに立たせ絵にうつす君がゆかたに柿の花ちる

ushi no ko wo
kokage ni tatase
e ni utsusu
kimi ga yukata ni
kaki no hana chiru

making a calf stand
under the shade of a tree
the picture drawn
is of you in a summer robe
with scattered persimmon petals

165

誰が筆に染めし扇ぞ去年までは白きをめでし君にやはあらぬ

ta ga fude ni
someshi Ōgi zo
kozo madewa
shiroki wo medeshi
kimi ni yawa aranu

who brushed
those letters on your fan
until last year
wasn't it you who
praised only white

166

おもざしの似たるにまたもまどひけりたはぶれますよ恋の神々

omozashi no
nitaru ni mata mo
madoikeri
tawabure masu yo
koi no kamigami

again
his similar features
are a delusion
you gods of love are
ever bolder tricksters

Myōjō, July, 1901.

167

五月雨に築土くづれし鳥羽殿のいぬゐの池におもだかさきぬ

samidare ni
tsuiji kuzureshi
tobadono no
inui no ike ni
omodaka sakinu

in summer rains
the mud wall crumbles
in the Toba Palace
arrowhead plants bloomed
in the northwest pond

Toba detached palace is a general term for the complex begun by Retired
Emperor Shirakawa in 1086, in the marshy belt south of the Heian capital
in Fushimi ward, Kyoto.
Omodaka - Arrowhead - *Sagittaria latifolia* is a plant found in the shallow
bogs in the area of this palace complex. The tubers on the roots were
edible. A raceme is composed of large flowers whorled by threes usually
divided into female flowers on the lower part and male on the upper.

168

つばくらの羽にしたたる春雨をうけてなでむかわが朝寝髪

tsubakura no
hane ni shitataru
harusame wo
ukete naden ka
waga asanegami

from a swallow's
feather is dripping
spring rain
shall I catch it to smooth
my late-morning hair

Tsubakura - H. r. gutturalis - barn swallow which has whitish underparts
and a broken breast band. Breast is chestnut with lower underparts more
pink-buff. The primary breeding range is Japan and Korea.

169
しら菊を折りてゑまひし朝すがた垣間みしつと人の書きこし

shiragiku wo
orite emaishi
asa sugata
kaimamishitsu to
hito no kakikoshi

a white chrysanthemum
you smiled as you snapped it off
in the morning
after catching a glimpse of me
somebody wrote this note

170
八つ口をむらさき緒もて我とめじひかばあたへむ三尺の袖

yatsuguchi wo
murasaki o mote
ware tomeji
hikaba ataen
san-jaku no sode

armpit slit
I won't sew up the kimono
with a purple thread
if you pull I'll give you
three feet of sleeve

171

春かぜに桜花ちる層塔のゆふべを鳩の羽に歌そめむ

harukazeni
sakurabana chiru
sōtō no
yūbe wo hato no
ha ni uta somen

a spring breeze
scatters cherry petals
in the pagoda
at dusk on a dove's feather
I will write a poem

Writing poems on leaves was the usual practice. Akiko makes the task
harder by writing on a feather.
Tekkan had written a tanka to a dove and Akiko replied. She did not
include the exchange but picked this tanka about the exchange.
Myōjō, July, 1901.

172

憎からぬねたみもつ子とききし子の垣の山吹歌うて過ぎぬ

nikukaranu
netami motsu ko to
kikishi ko no
kaki no yamabuki
utōte suginu

she's not so hateful
I heard of a girl who is
jealous of me
she passes while reciting
a poem about a hedge rose

The flower is the *yamabuki*, which if not trained up on a trellis can form a
thicket or hedge.

173

おばしまのその片袖ぞおもかりし鞍馬を西へ流れにし霞

obashima no
sono katasode zo
omokarishi
Kurama wo nishi e
nagare nishi kasumi

> on the railing
> just one sleeve was
> so heavy
> west of Kurama
> the mist floated

Mount Kurama is a mountain to the north-west of the city of Kyoto. It is
the birthplace of the Reiki practice, and is said to be the home of Sōjōbō,
King of the Tengu, who taught swordsmanship to Minamoto no
Yoshitsune.

174

ひとたびは神より更ににほひ高き朝をつつみし練の下襲

hitotabi wa
kami yori sarani
nioi takaki
asa wo tsutsumishi
neri no shitagasane

> once
> I was sweeter than god
> with the high scent
> of morning wrapped in
> underclothes of purest silk

Shitagasane were the underclothes the hem of which trailed along the
floor. Its length varied according to one's rank. After Kamakura Era
everyone wore short underclothes except the emperor.

113

SHIRAYURI - WHITE LILY

175

月の夜の蓮のおばしま君うつくしうら葉の御歌わすれはせずよ

tsuki no yo no
hasu no obashima
kimi utsukushi
uraba no miuta
wasure wa sezu yo

at night moonlight
on the lotus by the railing
you're so beautiful
I never forget your poem
written on top of a leaf

Though the section is called "White Lily," the first four poems are about lotus flowers. The poem refers to the time Tomiko – "White Lily" who was with Akiko and Tekkan at the Suminoe Temple when they took turns writing poems on lotus leaves.

176

たけの髪をとめ二人に月うすき今宵しら蓮色まどはずや

take no kami
otome futari ni
tsuki usuki
koyoi shirahasu
iro madowazu ya

two maidens
with hair as long as they are tall
in dim moonlight
are puzzled this evening
by the color of a white lotus

Written on a trip with Tekkan and Tomiko to the Suminoe Shrine on August 9, 1900.

177
荷葉なかば誰にゆるすの上の御句ぞ御袖片取るわかき師の君

hasu nakaba
dare ni yurusu no
kami no miku zo
misode katatoru
wakaki shi no kimi

centered in the lotus
who will he pass it to
the upper verse
my young teacher
holds back his sleeve

August 9, 1900 when Akiko, and Tomiko, and Tekkan stayed at the
Suminoe Shrine they played a capping game with tanka in which one
person wrote either the upper or the lower part and then handed the
partial poem to another to be finished. They were writing on lotus leaves.

178
おもひおもふ今のこころに分ち分かず君やしら萩われやしろ百合

omoi omou
ima no kokoro ni
wakachi wakazu
kimi ya sirahagi
ware ya siroyuri

thinking feeling
what now is in our hearts
shared but not shared
you are a bush clover
I am a white lily

Actually Tekkan called Tomiko "White Lily" and Akiko was "Bush
Clover."

179

いづれ君ふるさと遠き人の世ぞと御手はなちしは昨日の夕

izure kimi
furusato tōki
hito no yo zo to
mite hanachishi wa
kinō no yūbe

in any case
a hometown is far away
for human beings,
you said loosening your grip
yesterday evening

180

三たりをば世にうらぶれしはらからとわれ先づ云ひぬ西の京の宿

mitari wo ba
yo ni urabureshi
harakara to
ware mazu iinu
nishi no kyō no yado

those three people
so shabby in this world
are brother and sisters
I said from the beginning
at the inn west of Kyōto

November 5 – 7, 1900, Akiko, Tomiko, and Tekkan journeyed together to
Mt. Awata to see the fall colors. Each had problems with the world: Akiko
wanted to get away from home, Tomiko did not want to marry her father's
choice of husband, and Tekkan had been rejected by his wife's family so
she wanted to leave him.
Myōjō, November, 1900.

116

181

今宵まくら神にゆづらぬやは手なりたがはせまさじ白百合の夢

koyoi makura
kami ni yuzuranu
yawa te nari
tagawasemasaji
shirayuri no yume

tonight I won't hand
the pillow over to a god
to play into my hands
I don't betray the dream
of a white lily

182

夢にせめてせめてと思ひその神に小百合の露の歌ささやきぬ

yume ni semete
semete to omoi
sono kami ni
sayuri no tsuyu no
uta sasayakinu

at least in dreams
at the very least I think
that to god
the dewdrop of a tiny lily
whispered a poem

117

183

次のまのあま戸そとくるわれをよびて秋の夜いかに長きみぢかき

tsugi no ma no
amado soto kuru
ware wo yobite
aki no yo ika ni
nagaki mijikaki

as I softly
slid the anteroom's shutters
he called out
how was the autumn night
too long or too short

amado = the traditional Japanese shutter door that is slid open and closed.
The poem refers to the trip to Mt. Awata on November 5 – 7, 1900.
Myōjō, November, 1900.

184

友のあしのつめたかりきと旅の朝わかきわが師に心なくいひぬ

tomo no ashi no
tsumetakariki to
tabi no asa
wakaki waga shi ni
kokoronaku iinu

my friend's feet
were so cold in the morning
during our trip
I said thoughtlessly
to my young master

185
ひとまおきてをりをりもれし君がいきその夜しら梅だくと夢みし

hitoma okite
oriori moreshi
kimi ga iki
sono yo shiraume
daku to yume mishi

from one room away
occasionally I could overhear
your breathing
that night I dreamed
a white plum was embraced

On November 5, 1900, Akiko, Tomiko, and Tekkan went to Eikandō to view the colored leaves on Mt. Awata where they stayed in the Tsujino Inn. Tekkan had the main room and the two women slept together in an ante-chamber. Akiko's nickname for Tekkan was White Plum. *Myōjō*, November, 1900.

186
いはず聴かずただうなづきて別れけりその日は六日二人と一人

iwazu kikazu
tada unazukite
wakarekeri
sono hi wa muika
futari to hitori

wordless
you merely nod
at our parting
on the sixth day of the month
two together – one alone

This poem is a play with numbers.

187

もろ羽かはし掩ひしそれも甲斐なかりきうつくしの友西の京の秋

moroha kawashi
ooishi sore mo
kai nakariki
utsukushi no tomo
nishi no kyō no aki

with both wings
we protected her
it was of no use
my beautiful friend
west Kyōto in autumn

Another poem from the November 5 – 7 trip to Mt. Awata. Tekkan and
Akiko wanted to protect Tomiko from having to go through with the
marriage she did not want.
Myōjō, January, 1901.

188

星となりて逢はむそれまで思ひ出でなひとつふすまに聞きし
秋の声

hoshi to narite
awan soremade
omoiidena
hitotsu fusuma ni
kikishi aki no koe

becoming stars
when we meet then
do not recall
the paper door where we
heard the voice of autumn

189
人の世に才秀でたるわが友の名の末かなし今日秋くれぬ

hito no yo ni
sai hiidetaru
waga tomo no
na no sue kanashi
kyō aki kurenu

       in this world
    the excellent abilities
       of my friend
   will make her famous
   today her autumn left

190
星の子のあまりによわし袂あげて魔にも鬼にも勝たむと云へな

hoshi no ko no
amari ni yowashi
tamoto agete
ma ni mo oni ni mo
katan to ie na

     child of the stars
   you are much too weak
     to raise a sleeve
  unable to say I will beat
 either the devil or demons

At this time, November 5, 1900, Tomiko's father was insisting that she marry a distant relative she did not like. Akiko and Tekkan seemed to want to dissuade her from the marriage, but Akiko realized that if Tomiko married that would remove her from Tekkan's affections.

191

百合の花わざと魔の手に折らせおきて拾ひてだかむ神のこころか

yuri no hana
wazato ma no te ni
oraseokite
hiroite dakan
kami no kokoroka

lily flower
if the devil's hand
snaps it off
leave it alone for someone
else to pick up and embrace

192

しろ百合はそれその人の高きおもひおもわは艶ふ紅芙蓉とこそ

shiroyuri wa
sore sono hito no
takaki omoi
omowa wa niou
benifuyō to koso

a white lily
she is thus to that person
with lofty thoughts
however she is as alluring
as a red cotton rose too

A cotton rose is another name for a haibiscus.

193
さはいへどそのひと時よまばゆかりき夏の野しめし白百合の花

sa wa iedo
sono hitotoki yo
mabayukariki
natsu no no shimeshi
shirayuri no hana

no matter
what they said at the time
it was dazzling
when the summer field
was taken by white lilies

194
友は二十ふたつこしたる我身なりふさはずあらじ恋と伝へむ

tomo wa hatachi
futatsu koshitaru
waga mi nari
fusawazu araji
koi to tsutaen

my friend is 20
I am two years older
for me
it would be proper
to talk about love

195

その血潮ふたりは吐かぬちぎりなりき春を山蓼たづねますな君

sono chishio
futari wa hakanu
chigiri nariki
haru wo yamatade
tazune masuna kimi

that blood bond
between us cannot be broken
the promise was made
in spring do not even look
at the knotweed my dear

196

秋を三人椎の実なげし鯉やいづこ池の朝かぜ手と手つめたき

aki wo mitari
shii no mi nageshi
koi ya izuko
ike no asa kaze
te to te tsumetaki

last autumn
we three tossed acorns
to carp in the pond
where now in dawn wind
our touching hands are cold

197

かの空よ若狭は北よわれ載せて行く雲なきか西の京の山

kano sora yo
Wakasa wa kita yo
ware nosete
yuku kumo naki ka
nishi no kyō no yama

to that sky
of Wakasa in the north
I would climb
on a cloud if it would go there
from the mountain west of Kyoto

198

ひと花はみづから渓にもとめきませ若狭の雪に堪へむ紅

hito hana wa
mizukara tani ni
motome kimase
Wakasa no yuki ni
taen kurenai

that one flower
should come to the valley
on her own will
in spite of snow in Wakasa
her red color will never fade

199
「筆のあとに山居のさまを知りたまへ」人への人の文さりげなき

fude no atoni
yamai no sama wo
shiritamae
hito no hito eno
fumi sarigenaki

from my handwriting
you can guess my way of life
in the mountains
from person to person
this letter is only casual

200
京はもののつらきところと書きさして見おろしませる加茂の
河しろき

kyō wa mono no
tsuraki tokoro to
kakisashite
mioroshimaseru
kamo no kawa shiroki

Kyōto is
a place of torment for me
he wrote
then stopped to look down
on the pale Kamo River

201

恨みまつる湯におりしまの一人居を歌なかりきの君へだてあり

urami matsuru
yu ni orishi ma no
hitori-i wo
uta nakariki no
kimi hedate ari

it's so sad
to be in the bath
alone
no poem was written
and you are so distant

202

秋の衾あしたわびし身うらめしきつめたきためし春の京に得ぬ

aki no fusuma
ashita wabishi mi
urameshiki
tsumetaki tameshi
haru no Kyō ni en

autumn quilt
on a lonely morning
the bitterness
of that cold testing I got
in the Kyōto spring

203

わすれては谿へおりますうしろ影ほそき御肩に春の日よわき

wasurete wa
tani e orimasu
ushiro kage
hosoki mikata ni
haru no hi yowaki

forgetting
she had gone to the valley
a back
with your slender shoulders
in spring sunlight is so gentle

204

京の鐘この日このとき我れあらずこの日このとき人と人を泣きぬ

Kyō no kane
konohi kono toki
ware arazu
konohi konotoki
hito to hito wo nakinu

the bell in Kyōto
this day this time
I was not here
this day this time
we wept for her

205

琵琶の海山ごえ行かむいざと云ひし秋よ三人よ人そぞろなりし

Biwa no umi
yama goe yukan
iza to iishi
aki yo mitari yo
hito sozoro narishi

to Lake Biwa
let us go over the mountain
we said
three people in autumn
each with our own intentions

206

京の水の深み見おろし秋を人の裂きし小指の血のあと寒き

kyō no mizu no
fukami mioroshi
aki wo hito no
sakishi oyubi no
chi no ato samuki

Kyoto waters
looking down into the chill
someone in autumn
cut her little finger
to leave a blood mark

Memories of being with Tomiko and Tekkan in November, 1900. Tomiko
married in April, 1901, which made waiting for Tekkan to let her come to
Tokyo even harder.
Myōjō, May, 1901.

207

山蓼のそれよりふかきくれなゐは梅よはばかれ神にとがおはむ

yamatade no
sore yori fukaki
kurenai wa
ume yo habakare
kami ni toga owan

knotweed
a deeper red than
the plum
so be modest or the gods
will charge you with blame

This tanka was included in Akiko's letter of get-well written to him in September, 1900. Akiko had repeatedly asked Tekkan, her teacher, if it was permissible to put her real feelings into a tanka.

208

魔のまへに理想くだきしよわき子と友のゆふべをゆびさしますな

ma no mae ni
omoi kudakishi
yowaki ko to
tomo no yūbe wo
yubisashi masuna

before the devil
her ideals broken
the weak child
my friend of last evening
don't point the blame at her

This is about Tomiko's way of living. She gave up her ideal of being a poet and living when she decided to marry a man she did not love. In those days Japanese marriage was family-and-family tie, not man-and-woman tie. Usually the girls followed the traditional way, only some of the girls were brave enough to break off with their family and marry a man she loved. Akiko was one of them and Tomiko looked a coward from a brave person's view. So Akiko says Tomiko looks too weak to carry out her ideal way of living but you should not blame her as a coward.

209
魔のわざを神のさだめと眼をとぢし友の片手の花あやぶみぬ

ma no waza wo
kami no sadame to
me wo tojishi
tomo no katate no
hana ayabuminu

> devil's work
> but she says it destiny
> closing her eyes;
> the flower in her hand
> looks so fragile

Tomiko accepted her parents' suggestion and decided to marry. Akiko
thought it was a devil's work. But her friend said it was her fate or god's
decision and closed her eyes. Akiko was afraid that the flower in her hand
would be withered soon. I am not sure what the flower in her hand means.
It may be Tomiko's tanka, her talent, or the life as a tanka poet.
ayabuminu means to think or to be afraid that it will be in a difficult
situation or in hazard.

210
歌をかぞへその子この子にならふなのまだ寸ならぬ白百合の芽よ

uta wo kazoe
sono ko kono ko ni
narauna no
mada sun naranu
shirayuri no me yo

> listing the poems
> from this person or that one
> don't copy
> you are not even an inch
> of a white lily bud

131

HATACHI ZUMA –TWENTY-YEAR-OLD WIFE

211

露にさめて瞳もたぐる野の色よ夢のただちの紫の虹

tsuyu ni samete
hitomi motaguru
no no iro yo
yume no tadachi no
murasaki no niji

awaken to dew
I raise my eyes to
a field of color
lovely in the passing dream
a purple rainbow

212

やれ壁にチチアンが名はつらかりき湧く酒がめを夕に秘めな

yare kabe ni
chichian no na wa
tsurakariki
waku sakegame wo
yūbe ni hime na

on the shabby wall
Titian's art is hard to value
don't hide
the bottle of sake
so stimulating at dusk

Myōjō, July, 1901.

213
何となきただ一ひらの雲に見ぬみちびきさとし聖歌のにほひ

nani to naki
tada hito hira no
kumo ni minu
michibiki satoshi
seika no nioi

somehow
only a piece of cloud
showed me
the way to the teaching
with the scent of a hymn

214
神にそむきふたたびここに君と見ぬ別れの別れさいへ乱れじ

kami ni somuki
futatabi kokoni
kimi to min
wakare no wakare
sa ie midareji

to disobey god
again and now here
I meet you
the continual farewells
I say they don't upset me

215

淵の水になげし聖書を又もひろひ空仰ぎ泣くわれまどひの子

fuchi no mizu ni
nageshi seisho wo
matamo hiroi
sora aogi naku
ware madoi no ko

picking up again
the Bible I had thrown
in deep water
I look at the sky and weep
this child who lost her way

216

聖書だく子人の御親の墓に伏して弥勒の名をば夕に喚びぬ

seisho daku ko
hito no mioya no
haka ni fushite
miroku no na woba
yūbe ni yobinu

holding a Bible
a girl grovels before the tomb
of her lover's parents
the name of Maitreya
she calls in the evening

Maitreya is a bodhisattva – a saint - who in the Buddhist tradition is to
appear on earth to bring enlightenment at a time when the Dharma – law
or natural order will have been forgotten.

217

神ここに力をわびぬとき紅のにほひ興がるめしひの少女

kami kokoni
chikara wo wabinu
tokibeni no
nioi kyōgaru
meshii no otome

here God
laments a lack of power
liquid rouge
has the scent of love
even for this blind girl

218

痩せにたれかひなもる血ぞ猶わかき罪を泣く子と神よ見ますな

yasenitare
kaina moru chi zo
nao wakaki
tsumi wo naku ko to
kami yo mimasuna

thinner now
this arm's blood is
still young
God don't think
this child weeps for sins

219

おもはずや夢ねがはずや若人よもゆるくちびる君に映らずや

omowazu ya
yume negawazu ya
wakōdo yo
moyuru kuchibiru
kimi ni utsurazu ya

isn't it natural
to wish to fulfill a dream
young men
aren't they lovely
these burning lips?

220

君さらば巫山の春のひと夜妻またの世までは忘れゐたまへ

kimi saraba
Fuzan no haru no
hitoyozuma
mata no yo made wa
wasure itamae

your farewell
in the spring at Fuzan
I am a one-night wife
until we meet in heaven
thus please forget me

In a letter on February 2, 1901 from Akiko to Tekkan. He had ravished her and then left her with promises of marriage that he was not keeping. She threatened suicide if the situation did not change.

221
あまきにがき味うたがひぬ我を見てわかきひじりの流しにし涙

amaki nigaki
aji utagainu
ware wo mite
wakaki hijiri no
nagashinishi namida

sweet or bitter
how did the tears taste
looking at me
a young priest
falls into weeping

From a series of tanka on the subject of being alone on the holiday
Tanabata. *Tanabata* traditionally is held on the seventh night of the seventh
month. This is when the Herdsman, the star Altair , is allowed to cross the
Milky Way or River of Heaven, to visit his lover, Weaver Princess – the
star Vega. If it rains the lovers cannot meet. Wishes are written on slips of
paper hung on bamboo trees or twigs.
Myōjō October, 1900.

222
歌に名は相問はざりきさいへ一夜ゑにしのほかの一夜とおぼすな

uta ni na wa
ai towazariki
saie hitoyo
enishi no hoka no
hitoyo to obosuna

we didn't ask
whose poem it was
but that night
was a turn of fate
don't think it wasn't

223

水の香をきぬにおほひぬわかき神草には見えぬ風のゆるぎよ

mizu no ka wo
kinu ni ōinu
wakaki kami
kusa niwa mienu
kaze no yurugiyo

the scent of water
is covered by the robe
of the young god
in the grass one can't see
the sway of the wind

This tanka compares an almighty God with a powerless woman. The young god is able to cover the scent of water and block the wind. The woman in love with him knows neither the scent of water nor the movement of the breeze. The scent of water and the quiver of the breeze may be his affairs with other women.

224

ゆく水のざれ言きかす神の笑まひ御歯あざやかに花の夜あけぬ

yuku mizu no
zaregoto kikasu
kami no emai
miha azayakani
hana no yo akenu

flowing water
as we listen to jokes
god smiles
his glistening teeth are
flowers as night fades

225
百合にやる天の小蝶のみづいろの翅にしつけの糸をとる神

yuri ni yaru
ame no kochō no
mizu-iro no
hane ni shitsuke no
ito wo toru kami

      sending to a lily
   a little butterfly from heaven
       in pale blue
     the basting threads
    are removed by god

Japanese kimono always have basting threads after being cleaned. These
threads need to be removed before wearing it.
Myōjō, July, 1901.

226
ひとつ血の胸くれなゐの春のいのちひれふすかをり神もとめよる

hitotsu chi no
mune kurenai no
haru no inochi
hirefusu kaori
kami motomeyoru

     the same blood
   burning red in my chest
    is the life of spring
    god comes closer
  hungry for the lowly scent

227

わがいだくおもかげ君はそこに見む春のゆふべの黄雲のちぎれ

waga idaku
omokage kimi wa
soko ni min
haru no yūbe no
kigumo no chigire

I hold
an image of you
to see
in the spring evening
a bit of a golden cloud

228

むねの清水あふれてつひに濁りけり君も罪の子我も罪の子

mune no shimizu
afurete tsui ni
nigorikeri
kimi mo tsumi no ko
ware mo tsumi no ko

spring water
flowing over our chests
is now muddy
you are a boy of sin
I am a girl of sin

229
うらわかき僧よびさます春の窓ふり袖ふれて経くづれきぬ

urawaki
sō yobisamasu
haru no mado
furisode furete
kyō kuzure kinu

> so youthful
> the priest awakened
> in spring by a window
> a long-sleeved robe
> topples a pile of sutras

Myōjō, May, 1901.

230
今日を知らず智慧の小石は問はでありき星のおきてと別れにし朝

kyō wo shirazu
chie no koishi wa
towade ariki
hoshi no okite to
wakare nishi asa

> today I don't know
> the wisdom of a small stone
> nor can I ask
> the law of the stars tears
> us apart in the morning

231

春にがき貝多羅葉の名をききて堂の夕日に友の世泣きぬ

haru nigaki
baitarayō no
na wo kikite
dō no yūhi ni
tomo no yo nakinu

sad spring
the word "pattra" made me cry
in the temple at sunset
for the life of my friend
who had become a nun

Baitarayō is the word from the pronunciation of "pattra" which meant a
leaf of fan palm in ancient India. They engraved sutra on the *pattra* with a
needle.

232

ふた月を歌にただある三本樹加茂川千鳥恋はなき子ぞ

futatsuki wo
uta ni tada aru
Sanbongi
Kamogawa chidori
koi wa naki ko zo

for two months
there were only the poems
at Sanbongi
on Duck River are plovers
this girl is not in love

233
わかき子が乳の香まじる春雨に上羽を染めむ白き鳩われ

wakaki ko ga
chichi no ka majiru
harusame ni
uwaba wo somen
shiroki hato ware

the scent of
young girl's milk mingles
with spring rain
to dye the outer feathers
I the white dove

234
夕ぐれを花にかくるる小狐のにこ毛にひびく北嵯峨の鐘

yūgure wo
hana ni kakururu
kogitsune no
nikoge ni hibiku
Kita Saga no kane

at dusk
the flowers hide
a small fox
in its soft fur the bell
of North Saga rings

The original poem says, "a small fox is hidden by the flowers."

235

見しはそれ緑の夢のほそき夢ゆるせ旅人かたり草なき

mishi wa sore
midori no yume no
hosoki yume
yuruse tabibito
katarigusa naki

what I had
was a green dream
a thin dream
I am sorry traveler
I have no story to tell

236

胸と胸とおもひことなる松のかぜ友の頬を吹きぬ我頬を吹きぬ

mune to mune to
omoi kotonaru
matsu no kaze
tomo no hō wo fukinu
waga hō wo fukinu

chest to chest
though our feelings vary
a pine breeze
on my friend's cheeks
blows over my cheeks

237
野茨ををりて髪にもかざし手にもとり永き日野辺に君まちわびぬ

nobara orite
kami ni mo kazashi
te ni mo tori
nagaki hi nobe ni
kimi machiwabinu

I pick wild roses
some for my hair
others in my hand
struggling the long day
waiting for you in a field

238
春を説くなその朝かぜにほころびし袂だく子に君こころなき

haru wo tokuna
sono asakaze ni
hokorobishi
tamoto daku ko ni
kimi kokoronaki

don't tell me
about the spring of life
it's a morning wind
that ripped my precious sleeve
you are also thoughtless

Spring here means the spring of life and love and the sleeve is her heart.
She does not like to hear about love, for she wants to soothe her broken
heart. He is thoughtless to talk of love now.

239

春をおなじ急瀬さばしる若鮎の釣緒の細緒くれなゐならぬ

haru wo onaji
hayase sabashiru
waka-ayu no
tsuri-o no hoso-o
kurenai naranu

the same each spring
moving up the rapid stream
sweetfish fingerlings
thin lines of fishing strings
are not always red

The red fishing line may suggest "red string of fate" in the legendary
tales. They say the couples are tied with invisible red strings when they
are born. The tale came from old China where they say the future bride
and bridegroom are tied with a red rope at their ankles. In Japan the ankle
changed to the wrist or the little finger, and the rope changed to string. In
this poem young ayu fish goes up a river to mate but the fishing line may
hinder them from mating. So the lines could not be red.

240

みなぞこにけぶる黒髪ぬしや誰れ緋鯉のせなに梅の花ちる

minazoko ni
keburu kurokami
nushi ya dare
higoi no sena ni
ume no hana chiru

on the river bottom
dimly one can see black hair
whose is it?
on the back of a golden carp
plum blossoms scatter

241
秋を人のよりし柱にとがめあり梅にことかるきぬぎぬの歌

aki wo hito no
yorishi hashira ni
togame ari
ume ni kotokaru
kinuginu no uta

in autumn
she leaned against this post
it hurt me
when you made the plum poem
on the morning we parted

Taken from "Night Fragrance" - a series of poems exploring her jealousy.
The other woman's name was Masako and Tekkan called her "Plum
Flower."
Myōjō April, 1901.

242
京の山のこぞめしら梅人ふたりおなじ夢みし春と知りたまへ

kyō no yama no
kozome shiraume
hito futari
onaji yume mishi
haru to shiri tamae

on Kyōto's mountain
red and white plum blossoms
the two of us
had the same dream
those spring days

243
なつかしの湯の香梅が香山の宿の板戸によりて人まちし闇

natsukashi no
yu no ka ume ga ka
yama no yado no
itado ni yorite
hito machishi yami

a longing
for plum blossoms' scent at the spa
of the mountain inn
where I leaned on a wooden door
in darkness while I waited for you

244
詞にも歌にもなさじわがおもひその日そのとき胸より胸に

kotoba nimo
uta nimo nasaji
waga omoi
sono hi sono toki
mune yori mune ni

neither the prose
nor the poem will tell
my feelings
that day that time
from heart to heart

Myōjō October, 1900.

245
歌にねて昨夜梶の葉の作者見ぬうつくしかりき黒髪の色

uta ni nete
yobe Kaji no Ha no
sakusha minu
utsukushikariki
kurokami no iro

> sleeping on the poems
> of the *Mulberry Leaf* last night
> I saw the author
> who was beautiful
> with black-colored hair

Kaji-jo, known as the Lady of the Mulberry Leaf – a tea house in the Gion area of Kyoto that was the gathering place for artists and writers, wrote tanka. Her collection of tanka, published between 1704 – 1710, was a huge influence on Akiko's writing after a dream Akiko had that the lady appeared to her.
Myōjō, October, 1900.

246
下京や紅屋が門をくぐりたる男かわゆし春の夜の月

Shimogyō ya
beniya ga kado wo
kuguritaru
otoko kawayushi
haru no yo no tsuki

> a shopping district
> at the door of a cosmetic shop
> passing through
> was a handsome man
> the moon on a spring night

Shimogyō is one of the eleven wards in the city of Kyoto, in Kyoto Prefecture, Japan. First established in 1879, it has been merged and split, and took on its present boundaries in 1955, with the establishment of a separate Minami-ku. Shijō Kawaramachi intersection, is the busiest shopping district in the city.

247

枝折戸あり紅梅さけり水ゆけり立つ子われより笑みうつくしき

shiorido ari
kōbai sakeri
mizu yukeri
tatsu ko ware yori
emi utsukushiki

there is a wicker gate
where the red plum blooms
by flowing water
stands a girl whose smile
is more beautiful than mine

248

しら梅は袖に湯の香は下のきぬにかりそめながら君さらばさらば

shiraume wa
sode ni yu no ka wa
shita no kinu
karisome nagara
kimisaraba saraba

with white plum blossoms
in my sleeve is the scent of hot water
in our underwear
our parting is only temporary
good-bye, good-bye, dear

249
二十とせの我世の幸はうすかりきせめて今見る夢やすかれな

hata tose no
waga yo no sachi wa
usukariki
semete ima miru
yume yasukarena

for 20 years
the happiness in my life
was very slim
at least in this moment
may I dream of peace

250
二十とせのうすきいのちのひびきありと浪華の夏の歌に泣きし君

hatatose no
usuki inochi no
hibiki ari to
Naniwa no natsu no
uta ni nakishi kimi

twenty years
of an unhappy life
they echo
in the poem from Naniwa
that summer when you wept

251

かつぐきぬにその間の床の梅ぞにくき昔がたりを夢に寄する君

katsugu kinu ni
sono ma no toko no
ume zo nikuki
mukashigatari wo
yume ni yosuru kimi

wearing silk clothes
in the alcove of our room
I hated the plum
you put the old stories
under the veil of dreams

252

それ終に夢にはあらぬそら語り中のともしびいつ君きえし

sore tsuini
yume niwa aranu
soragatari
naka no tomoshibi
itsu kimi kieshi

after all
it was not a dream
but in imagination
the light has faded
when did you go away

253

君ゆくとその夕ぐれに二人して柱にそめし白萩の歌

kimi yuku to
sono yūgure ni
futari shite
hashira ni someshi
shira hagi no uta

you were going
to leave that evening
we two
wrote on the pillar a poem
about the white bush clover

When Tekkan met both Akiko and Tomiko secretly at an inn near Osaka, he left before the two women did. It is assumed that the action in this poem then occurred in his absence. White bush clover or *lezepeda*, is the tradition symbol for autumn, for farewells, for sadness and regrets and was Tekkan's nickname for Akiko.

254

なさけあせし文みて病みておとろへてかくても人を猶恋ひわたる

nasake aseshi
fumi mite yamite
otoroete
kakute mo hito wo
nao koi wataru

I see in his letter
sympathy fades for my illness
still declining
even so this person
will love him forever

255

夜の神のあともとめよるしら綾の鬢の香朝の春雨の宿

yo no kami no
ato motomeyoru
shira aya no
bin no ka asa no
harusame no yado

the night god
chases the remainder
on damask
the scent of morning hair
at the inn in spring rain

256

その子ここに夕片笑みの二十びと虹のはしらを説くに隠れぬ

sonoko kokoni
yū kataemi no
hatachi bito
niji no hashira wo
toku ni kakuren

that girl here
smiling in the evening
is twenty
if you seduce her
she hides from you

257

このあした君があげたるみどり子のやがて得む恋うつくしかれな

kono ashita
kimi ga agetaru
midorigo no
yagate e'n koi
utsukushikare na

this morning
to you was born
a baby
may it soon win
a beautiful love

September 23, 1900, Tekkan Yosano's common-law wife, Takino, gave birth to a son they named Atsumu. Akiko sent this poem in a letter of congratulations.

258

恋の神にむくいまつりし今日の歌ゑにしの神はいつ受けまさむ

koi no kami ni
mukui matsurishi
kyō no uta
enishi no kami wa
itsu ukemasan

to the god of love
I offered a poem of
homage today
when will you accept it
my god go-between

259
かくてなほあくがれますか真善美わが手の花はくれなゐよ君

kakute nao
akugaremasu ka
shin zen bi
waga te no hana wa
kurenai yo kimi

in this way
are you still yearning for truth,
goodness and beauty?
this flower in my hand
is a dazzling red my love

260
くろ髪の千すぢの髪のみだれ髪かつおもひみだれおもひみだるる

kuro kami no
chi suji no kami no
midaregami
katsu omoimidare
omoididaruru

black hair
a thousand strands of hair
tangled
disturbs my heart
tangled with memories

261
そよ理想おもひにうすき身なればか朝の露草人ねたかりし

so yo risō
omoi ni usuki
mi nareba ka
asa no tsuyukusa
hito netakarishi

it is a dream
to flower for long
or lack of love
a dayflower in the morning
is jealous of the humans

Since the dayflower blooms only one day, one can think that it may be jealous of human beings who bloom with love with each other for a long time.

262
とどめあへぬそぞろ心は人しらむくづれし牡丹さぎぬに紅き

todome aenu
sozoro gokoro wa
hito shiran
kuzureshi botan
saginu ni akaki

insuppressible
my restless mind
you may know
the crushed peony
is red against silk clothes

263

あらざりきそは後の人のつぶやきし我には永久のうつくしの夢

arazariki
so wa nochi no hito no
tsubuyakishi
ware ni wa towa no
utsukushi no yume

it can't be
that later he was the one who
murmured
my future was
a beautiful dream

The word *tose* was later corrected to *towa*.
Myōjō July, 1901.

264

行く春の一弦一柱におもひありさいへ火かげのわが髪ながき

yuku haru no
hito wo hito ji ni
omoi ari
sa ie hokage no
waga kami nagaki

spring is passing
each string and bridge of the harp
is so dear to me
in the flickering light
my hair is long

265

のらす神あふぎ見するに瞼おもきわが世の闇の夢の小夜中

norasu kami
aogimisuru ni
mabuta omoki
waga yo no yami no
yume no sayonaka

> what's god saying
> when I try to look upwards
> heavy eyelids
> see my life of darkness
> as in a dream of midnight

266

そのわかき羊は誰に似たるぞの瞳の御色野は夕なりし

sono wakaki
hitsuji wa dare ni
nitaru zo no
hitomi no miiro
no wa yū narishi

> who is it
> that lamb reminds me of
> someone
> your eyes asked me
> on the evening field

267

あえかなる白きうすものまなじりの火かげの栄の咀はしき君

aeka naru
shiroki usumono
manajiri no
hokage no hae no
norowashiki kimi

so fragile
in a sheer white robe
at the corner of my eye
the brightness of the light
oh, you embarrass me!

268

紅梅にそぞろゆきたる京の山叔母の尼すむ寺は訪はざりし

kōbai ni
sozoroyukitaru
Kyō no yama
oba no ama sumu
tera wa towazarishi

under red plums
I strolled along on the mountain
above Kyōto
my aunt the nun lives
in a temple I did not visit

269
くさぐさの色ある花によそはれし棺のなかの友うつくしき

kusa gusa no
iro aru hana ni
yosowareshi
hitsugi no naka no
tomo utsukushiki

the grasses
offer the color of flowers
adorned
with them in a coffin
my friend is beautiful

270
五つとせは夢にあらずよみそなはせ春に色なき草ながき里

itsu tose wa
yume ni arazu yo
misonawase
haru ni iro naki
kusa nagaki sato

five years
are not in a dream
look at the village
with long grasses in spring
without flowers

271

すげ笠にあるべき歌と強ひゆきぬ若葉よ薫れ生駒葛城

sugegasa ni
arubeki uta to
shiyukinu
wakaba yo kaore
Ikoma Katsuragi

a grass hat
goes with these poems
I had to come
to smell the young leaves
in Ikoma Katsuragi

272

裾たるる紫ひくき根なし雲牡丹が夢の真昼しづけき

suso taruru
murasaki hikuki
nenashi gumo
botan ga yume no
mahiru shizukeki

trailing in the sky
a low purple cloud
is rootless
the dream of a peony
in the calm of midday

273

紫のわが世の恋のあさぼらけ諸手のかをり追風ながき

murasaki no
waga yo no koi no
asaborake
morode no kaori
oikaze nagaki

the purple
in my life is love
at dawn
the fragrance in my hands
is that of a long fair wind

Shōtenchi, August, 1901

274

このおもひ真昼の夢と誰か云ふ酒のかをりのなつかしき春

kono omoi
mahiru no yume to
tare ka iu
sake no kaori no
natsukashiki haru

this feeling
is a dream at midday
says someone
with scent of sake
in my beloved spring

275

みどりなるは学びの宮とさす神にいらへまつらで摘む夕すみれ

midori naru wa
manabi no miya to
sasu kami ni
irae matsurade
tsumu yū sumire

the green is
a palace of study
when god points
I do not answer him
just pick the evening violets

276

そら鳴りの夜ごとのくせぞ狂ほしき汝よ小琴よ片袖かさむ
（琴に）

soranari no
yogoto no kuse zo
kuruoshiki
nare yo ogoto yo
katasode kasan
(koto ni)

your habit
of making false sounds every night
makes me crazy
so my dear little harp
I will sleep with you
(to the harp)

Myōjō, July, 1901.

277

ぬしえらばず胸にふれむの行く春の小琴とおぼせ眉やはき君
　（琴のいらへて）

(koto no iraete)
nushi erabazu
mune ni furen no
yuku haru no
ogoto to obose
mayu yawaki kimi

(the harp replies)

accepting as a lover
anyone who presses me to her chest
to pass the spring
your little harp thinks only of
you with your soft eyebrows

Myōjō, July, 1901.

278

去年ゆきし姉の名よびて夕ぐれの戸に立つ人をあはれと思ひぬ

kozo yukishi
ane no na yobite
yūgure no
to ni tatsu hito wo
aware to omoinu

dead for a year
my elder sister's name
called at dusk
outside my door by him
whom I have so pitied

Akiko's half-sister, Hana, had recently died. A cousin who had loved her
before her marriage is the man in the poem.
Myōjō, August, 1900.

279

十九のわれすでに菫を白く見し水はやつれぬはかなかるべき

tsuzu no ware
sudeni sumire wo
shiroku mishi
mizu wa yatsurenu
hakanakaru beki

I am nineteen
already to me the violets
look white
the river is so low
life becomes fragile

280

ひと年をこの子のすがた絹に成らず画の筆すてて詩にかへし君

hitotose wo
kono ko no sugata
kinu ni narazu
e no fude sutete
shi ni kaeshi kimi

for one year
you tried drawing this girl on silk
without success
throwing away the brush sketches
you've decided to make poem

281

白きちりぬ紅きくづれぬ床の牡丹五山の僧の口おそろしき

shiroki chirinu
akaki kuzurenu
yuka no botan
gozan no sō no
kuchi osoroshiki

> whiteness scattered
> and the redness crumbled
> peonies on the floor
> of Five Mountain temples
> the priests' cruel debates

Myōjō, July, 1901.

282

今日の身に我をさそひし中の姉小町のはてを祈れと去にぬ

kyō no mi ni
ware wo sasoishi
naka no ane
komachi no hate wo
inore to ininu

> second elder sister
> who made me as I am
> told me to pray
> for beauty at her end
> then she passed away

283

秋もろし春みじかしをまどひなく説く子ありなば我れ道きかむ

aki moroshi
haru mijikashi wo
madoi naku
toku ko arinaba
ware michi kika'n

autumn is brittle
and spring is short
if without hesitation
one could explain this
I'd be his disciple

284

さそひ入れてさらばと我手はらひます御衣のにほひ闇やはらかき

sasoi-irete
saraba to waga te
haraimasu
mikeshi no nioi
yami yawarakaki

after tempting me
you brush aside my hand
with a *good-by*
the fragrance of your robe
in the velvety darkness

285

病みてこもる山の御堂に春くれぬ今日文ながき絵筆とる君

yamite komoru
yama no midō ni
haru kuren
kyō fumi nagaki
efude toru kimi

illness keeps me
in a mountain shrine
the spring sun sets
a long letter reaches today
from you with a paintbrush

Myōjō, July, 1901.

286

河ぞひの門小雨ふる柳はら二人の一人めす馬しろき

kawazoi no
kado kosame furu
yanagi hara
futari no hitori
mesu uma shiroki

along the river
light rain falls on the gate
at a willow field
one of the couple
is on a white mare

287

歌は斯くよ血ぞゆらぎしと語る友に笑まひを見せしさびしき思

uta wa kaku yo
chi zo yuragishi to
kataru tomo ni
emai wo miseshi
sabishiki omoi

a poem should
make one's blood quake
a friend said
my smile showed
the lonely feeling

288

とおもへばぞ垣をこえたる山ひつじとおもへばぞの花よわりなの

to omoebazo
kaki wo koetaru
yamahitsuji
to omoebazo no
hana yowarinano

positive thinking
the fence is climbed
by a mountain sheep
with thinking so a flower
tries not to wither

289
庭下駄に水をあやぶむ花あやめ鋏にたらぬ力をわびぬ

niwageta ni
mizu wo ayabumu
hana ayame
hasami ni taranu
chikara wo wabinu

the garden clogs
make me slip in water
where irises bloom
pity I am powerless
to cut them with scissors

290
柳ぬれし今朝門すぐる文づかひ青貝ずりのその箱ほそき

yanagi nureshi
kesa kado suguru
fumizukai
aogaizuri no
sono hako hosoki

the willow is wet
this morning by the gate
the courier's
narrow box is iridescent
inlaid with abalone shells

A *Fumizukai* here is not today's postman. He keeps a letter of some high-ranked person and delivers it to the other high-ranked person. The letter was kept in a decorated box.

291

「いまさらにそは春せまき御胸なり」われ眼をとぢて御手にすがりぬ

imasara ni
so wa haru semaki
mimune nari
ware me wo tojite
mite ni sugarinu

it is therefore
thoughtless of you
to say so now
closing my eyes
I cling to his hand

292

その友はもだえのはてに歌を見ぬわれを召す神きぬ薄黒き

sono tomo wa
modae no hate ni
uta wo minu
ware wo mesu kami
kinu usuguroki

that friend
who at the end of her agony
found poetry
my invitation to die
wears black silk

293
そのなさけかけますな君罪の子が狂ひのはてを見むと云ひたまへ

sono nasake
kakemasuna kimi
tsumi no ko ga
kurui no hate wo
mi'n to iitamae

even if you
don't have pity on me
a girl of sin
do tell her how
her crazy life will end

294
いさめますか道ときますかさとしますか宿世のよそに血を召しま
せな

isamemasu ka
michi tokimasu ka
satoshimasu ka
sukuse no yoso ni
chi wo meshi mase na

do you
reason with me
persuade or admonish
ignore our past
just take my blood

295

もろかりしはかなかりしと春のうた焚くにこの子の血ぞあま
り若き

morokarishi
hakanakarishi to
haru no uta
taku ni kono ko no
chi zo amari wakaki

it was fragile
a short-lived spring poem
the blood of this girl
is much too young
to be cremated

296

夏やせの我やねたみの二十妻里居の夏に京を説く君

natsuyase no
ware ya netami no
hatachi zuma
satoi no natsu ni
kyō wo toku kimi

summer loss of weight
still I am an envious wife
of twenty years
a summer staying in my parents' home
while you seduce someone in Kyoto

297
こもり居に集の歌ぬくねたみ妻五月のやどの二人うつくしき

komorii ni
shū no uta nuku
netami zuma
satsuki no yado no
futari utsukushiki

staying indoors
culling over my poems
as a jealous wife
still in our house in May
we are beautiful together

MAIHIME – DANCING GIRL

298

人に侍る大堰の水のおばしまにわかきうれひの袂の長き

hito ni haberu
ōi no mizu no
obashima ni
wakaki urei no
tamoto no nagaki

serving him
by the waters of the Oi River
at the railing
young in her grief
the one in long sleeves

299

くれなゐの扇に惜しき涙なりき嵯峨のみぢか夜暁寒かりし

kurenai no
ōgi ni oshiki
namida nariki
Saga no mijikayo
ake samukarishi

on a red fan
dropped wistful tears
in Saga
the night was too short
the dawn too cold

300
朝を細き雨に小鼓おほひゆくだんだら染の袖ながき君

asa wo hosoki
ame ni kotsuzumi
ōi yuku
dandara zome no
sode nagaki kimi

light morning rain
the small drum is covered
when you leave
by the colorful stripes
of your long sleeve

301
人にそひて今日京の子の歌をきく祇園清水春の山まろき

hito ni soite
kyō Kyō no ko no
uta wo kiku
Gion Kiyomizu
haru no yama maroki

coming with him
today to Kyoto this girl
listens to a song
in the Gion district spring
mountains are peaceful

302
くれなゐの襟にはさめる舞扇酔のすさびのあととめられな

kurenai no
eri ni hasameru
maiōgi
yoi no susabi no
ato tomerarena

her red collar
catches a fan for dancing
don't let him
leave a mark of mischief
when he is tipsy

303
桃われの前髪ゆへるくみ紐やときいろなるがことたらぬかな

momoware no
maegami yueru
kumihimo ya
toki iro naru ga
kototaranu kana

the hairstyle
for doing up the front
with braided cord
the pale pink color
is not exciting enough

304
浅黄地に扇ながしの都染め九尺のしごき袖よりも長き

asagiji ni
ōgi nagashi no
miyakozome
kushaku no shigoki
sode yori mo nagaki

on a yellow background
the pattern of flowing fans
dyed in Kyoto
the nine foot ribbon sash
is longer than my sleeves

305
四条橋おしろいあつき舞姫のぬかささやかに撲つ夕あられ

Shijō bashi
oshiroi atsuki
maihime no
nuka sasayakani
utsu yū arare

on Shijō bridge
in heavy make-up
a dancer's
brow lightly struck
by evening hail

306

さしかざす小傘に紅き揚羽蝶小褄とる手に雪ちりかかる

sashikazasu
ogasa ni akaki
ageha-chō
kozuma toru te ni
yuki chirikakaru

holding up
a small umbrella with a red
butterfly
on the robe's hem in her hand
the snow is falling

Since dancers and geisha wear long kimono that trail on the floor, they must lift up the hem when they walk.

307

舞姫のかりね姿ようつくしき朝京くだる春の川舟

maihime no
karine sugata yo
utsukushiki
asa Kyō kudaru
haru no kawabune

a dancing girl
even while napping she
is beautiful
in a riverboat on a spring morning
going down to Kyōto

308
紅梅に金糸のぬひの菊づくし五枚かさねし襟なつかしき

kōbai ni
kinshi no nui no
kikuzukushi
gomai kasaneshi
eri natsukashiki

red plum
various chrysanthemums
stitched with gold
the five layered collar
I miss so much

309
舞ぎぬの袂に声をおほひけりここのみ闇の春の廻廊

maiginu no
tamoto ni koe wo
ōikeri
koko no mi yami no
haru no watadono

a dancing robe
with its sleeve my cry
is covered
here in dark corridor
of the spring palace

310

まこと人を打たれむものかふりあげし袂このまま夜をなに舞はむ

makoto hito wo
utare'n mono ka
furiageshi
tamoto kono mama
yo wo nani mawa'n

truly
how can I beat you
raised overhead
with the sleeve as it is
what shall I dance tonight

311

三たび四たびおなじしらべの京の四季おとどの君をつらしと
思ひぬ

mitabi yotabi
onaji shirabe no
Kyō no shiki
otodo no kimi wo
tsurashi to omoinu

three or four times
the same melody of Kyōto
in four seasons
as a high-ranking person
you were cruel I thought

312
あでびとの御膝へおぞやおとしけり行幸源氏の巻絵の小櫛

adebito no
mihiza e ozoya
otoshikeri
Miyuki Genji no
emaki no ogushi

in a nobleman's lap
I boldly dropped
a small comb
with a pattern from story 29 in
The Tale of Genji picture scroll

Later in her life, Akiko would translate the complete version of *The Tale of Genji* into modern Japanese. While she was a girl she read the tales very often. Once she began writing tanka for each chapter she was surprised how easily the tanka flowed to her. This experience gave her the idea that she could write tanka.

313
しろがねの舞の花櫛おもくしてかへす袂のままならぬかな

shirogane no
mai no hanagushi
omokushite
kaesu tamoto no
mamanaranu kana

platinum comb
with floral decoration
for dancing
it's too heavy to let me turn
the sleeve as I want

314

四とせまへ鼓うつ手にそそがせし涙のぬしに逢はれむ我か

yotose mae
tsuzumi utsu te ni
sosogaseshi
namida no nushi ni
aware'n ware ka

four years ago
on the hand tapping the drum
I let him
pour out his tears
how can I meet him now

315

おほつづみ抱へかねたるその頃よ美き衣きるをうれしと思ひし

ōtsuzumi
kakae kanetaru
sono koro yo
yoki kinu kiru wo
ureshi to omoishi

the knee drum
was hard to hold
in those days
wearing the lovely robe
I thought I was happy

316
われなれぬ千鳥なく夜の川かぜに鼓拍子をとりて行くまで

ware narenu
chidori naku yo no
kawakaze ni
tsuzumibyōshi wo
torite yuku made

being used to
the cry of plovers on a night
of river winds
I take a walk even now
with drum-tapping rhythm

317
いもうとの琴には惜しきおぼろ夜よ京の子こひし鼓のひと手

imōto no
koto ni wa oshiki
oboroyo yo
Kyō no ko koishi
tsuzumi no hito te

the younger sister
so good on the harp
on the hazy moon night
misses a girl in Kyoto
the hand tapping the drum

185

318

よそほひし京の子すゑて絹のべて絵の具とく夜を春の雨ふる

yosooishi
kyō no ko suete
kinu nobete
enogu toku yo wo
haru no ame fure

beautifully dressed
the girl of Kyoto lies down
the stretched silk
colors dissolve in a night
of falling spring rain

319

そのなさけ今日舞姫に強ひますか西の秀才が眉よやつれし

sono nasake
kyō maihime ni
shiimasuka
nishi no susai ga
mayu yo yatsureshi

your love
is it forced on the Kyoto dancer
that bright person
of the western Japan
who looks so haggard

SHUNSHI – SPRING HEART

320

いとせめてもゆるがままにもえしめよ斯くぞ覚ゆる暮れて行く春

ito semete
moyuru ga mama ni
moeshime yo
kaku zo oboyuru
kurete yuku haru

> at least
> let my love flare up
> as it does
> so I think in spring
> coming to an end

Myōjō, July, 1901.

321

春みじかし何に不滅の命ぞとちからある乳を手にさぐらせぬ

haru mijikashi
nani ni fumetsu no
inochi zo to
chikara aru chi wo
te ni sagurasenu

> spring is short
> so what remains in life
> that is everlasting
> I let his hands grope for
> my powerful breasts

One tanka from the series "Scarlett Strings."
Myōjō, May, 1901.

322

夜の室に絵の具かぎよる懸想の子太古の神に春似たらずや

yo no muro ni
enogu kagiyoru
kesō no ko
taiko no kami ni
haru nitarazu ya

in the night room
drawn by the smell of paint
the lovesick child
doesn't he look like
an ancient god in spring

Myōjō, July, 1901.

323

そのはてにのこるは何と問ふな説くな友よ歌あれ終の十字架

sono hate ni
nokoru wa nani to
tou na toku na
tomo yo uta are
tsui no jūjika

in the end
what will remain
don't ask nor persuade
make a poem my friend
the cross is at the very end

324
わかき子が胸の小琴の音を知るや旅ねの君よたまくらかさむ

wakaki ko ga
mune no ogoto no
ne wo shiru ya
tabine no kimi yo
tamakura kasa'n

does a young girl
know the sound of a harp
against a breast
traveler my arms
will cradle you

325
松かげにまたも相見る君とわれゑにしの神をにくしとおぼすな

matsukage ni
mata mo aimiru
kimi to ware
enishi no kami wo
nikushi to obosu na

in pine shadow
we meet again
you and I
please don't hate
the god go-between

On August 15, 1900, Akiko met Tekkan on Takashi Beach with a group of writers. This was her response to a poem in which he had written, "I'll not forget." Akiko borrowed several words from Tekkan's tanka expressings friendship to turn them around to refer to love.

189

326

きのふをば千とせの前の世とも思ひ御手なほ肩に有りとも思ふ

kinō oba
chi tose no mae no
yo tomo omoi
mite nao kata ni
ari tomo omou

yesterday seems
a thousand years ago
even so
I feel your hand
on my shoulder

327

歌は君酔ひのすさびと墨ひかばさても消ゆべしさても消ぬべし

uta wa kimi
yoi no susabi to
sumi hikaba
satemo kiyubeshi
satemo kenubeshi

your poem
was only drunken fun
crossing it out
will vanish it from your mind
it will never vanish from mine

328

神よとはにわかきまどひのあやまちとこの子の悔ゆる歌きき
ますな

kami yo towani
wakaki madoi no
ayamachi to
kono ko no kuyuru
uta kikimasuna

well god
forever young in confusion
the mistakes
of this girl are regretted
never listen to the poem

329

湯あがりを御風めすなのわが上衣ゑんじむらさき人うつくしき

yuagari wo
mikaze mesuna no
waga uwagi
enjimurasaki
hito utsukushi

after the bath
not to catch a cold I offered
my jacket
with its dark red color
made him beautiful

191

330

さればとておもにうすぎぬかつぎなれず春ゆるしませ中の小屏風

sareba tote
omo ni usuginu
katsugi narezu
haru yurushi mase
naka no kobyōbu

not yet used to it
I cover my face with thin silk
allow me
to put this small screen
between us in spring

331

しら綾に鬢の香しみし夜着の襟そむるに歌のなきにしもあらず

shira aya ni
bin no ka shimishi
yogi no eri
somuru ni uta no
nakinishimo arazu

white fabric
keeps the scent of your hair
on the quilt's edge
it is impossible not to
write a poem of emotion

332

夕ぐれの霧のまがひもさとしなりき消えしともしび神うつくしき

yūgure no
kiri no magai mo
satoshi nariki
kieshi tomoshibi
kami utsukushiki

the foggy night
with its turbulence
was an omen
when the light's gone
my god is beautiful

333

もゆる口になにを含まむぬれといひしひとのをゆびの血は涸
れはてぬ

moyuru kuchi ni
nani wo fukuman
nure to iishi
hito no oyubi no
chi wa karehatenu

to my burning mouth
what have I kept that I
should apply
the blood from your
little finger is all dried

In the September issue of *Myōjō*, Tekkan had written: "Kyōto lip rouge /
does not become you / I've bit / my little finger so my blood / can color
your mouth with the heading of "To Akiko" and this was her reply three
months later.
Myōjō, December, 1900.

334

人の子の恋をもとむる唇に毒ある蜜をわれぬらむ願ひ

hito no ko no
koi wo motomuru
kuchibiru ni
doku aru mitsu wo
ware nuran negai

being human
a child of love seeking
these lips
I want to smear on them
poisonous honey

335

ここに三とせ人の名を見ずその詩よまず過ごすはよわきよわ
き心なり

koko ni mitose
hito no na wo mizu
sono shi yomazu
sugosu wa yowaki
yowaki kokoro nari

for three years
I have not seen his name
nor read his poems
that time passing exposes
my weak, weak heart

Myōjō March, 1901.

336
梅の渓の靄くれなゐの朝すがた山うつくしき我れうつくしき

ume no tani no
moya kurenai no
asa sugata
yama utsukushiki
ware utsukushiki

a valley of plums
with a deep crimson haze
at dawn
the mountain is beautiful
as I am beautiful

337
ぬしや誰ねぶの木かげの釣床の網のめもるる水色のきぬ

nushi ya tare
nebu no kokage no
tsuridoko no
ami no me moruru
mizuiro no kinu

whose is it
in the shade of a silk tree
escaping from
the hammock's mesh
this light blue garment

Written on August 6, 1900, at Takashi Beach on the given topic of clothes.

338

歌に声のうつくしかりし旅人の行手の村の桃しろかれな

uta ni koe no
utsukushikarishi
tabibito no
yukute no mura no
momo shirokarena

singing
in a beautiful voice
the traveler
left for a village
may their peaches be white

339

朝の雨につばさしめりし鶯を打たむの袖のさだすぎし君

asa no ame ni
tubasa shimerishi
uguisu wo
utan no sode no
sada sugishi kimi

morning rain
wets the wings of
a warbler
though you tried to hit it
your sleeve missed a chance

340

御手ずからの水にうがひしそれよ朝かりし紅筆歌かきてやまむ

mitezukara no
mizu ni ugaishi
sore yo asa
karishi benifude
uta kakite yaman

your own hands
rinsed with water
on that morning
I borrow the rouge brush
only for writing poems

341

春寒のふた日を京の山ごもり梅にふさはぬわが髪の乱れ

harusamu no
futahi wo Kyō no
yamagomori
ume ni fusawanu
waga kami no midare

in a cold spring
we retreated for two days
in the Kyoto hills
the tangles of my hair
out of place with the plum

January 9 – 11, 1901, Akiko and Tekkan returned to Mt. Awata for two
days alone at the inn where they had stayed with Tomiko in autumn.
Seiko, March, 1901.

342
歌筆を紅にかりたる尖凍てぬ西のみやこの春さむき朝

utafude wo
beni ni karitaru
saki itenu
nishi no miyako no
haru samuki asa

the writing brush
borrowed to apply rouge
had its tip frozen
in the western capital
spring's dawn chill

Seiko, March, 1901.

343
春の宵をちひさく撞きて鐘を下りぬ二十七段堂のきざはし

haru no yoi wo
chiisaku tsukite
kane wo orinu
nijūshichi dan
dō no kizahashi

a spring evening
with a small push
of the bell
I came down
27 steps of the temple

344
手をひたし水は昔にかはらずとさけぶ子の恋われあやぶみぬ

te wo hitashi
mizu wa mukashi ni
kawarazu to
sakebu ko no koi
ware ayabuminu

soaking her hand
that day in the water
it doesn't change
the girl in love cried
but I doubt it

345
病むわれにその子五つのをととなり or
をととなりつたなの笛をあはれと聞く夜

yamu ware ni
sono ko itsutsu no
wototo nari
tsutana no fue wo
aware to kiku yo

while I was sick
a five year old child
tries to be a man
his unskilled flute playing
moves me a lot at night

346

とおもひてぬひし春着の袖うらにうらみの歌は書かさせますな

to omoite
nuishi harugi no
sodeura ni
urami no uta wa
kakasase masuna

thinking of you
I sewed your spring robe
on the sleeve lining
don't let me write
a poem of spite

347

かくて果つる我世さびしと泣くは誰ぞしろ桔梗さく伽藍のうらに

kakute hatsuru
waga yo sabishi to
naku wa ta zo
shiro kikyō saku
garan no ura ni

thus my life ends
how lonely it all is
who is crying
among white bellflowers
behind the temple

348
人とわれおなじ十九のおもかげをうつせし水よ石津川の流れ

hito to ware
onaji jūku no
omokage wo
utsuseshi mizu yo
Ishizu gawa no nagare

you and I
both nineteen
our images
seen in the water
flowing in Ishizu River

349
卯の花を小傘にそへて褄とりて五月雨わぶる村はずれかな

unohana wo
ogasa ni soete
tsuma torite
samidare waburu
mura hazure kana

holding up deutzia
and a small umbrella
with the kimono's hem
rain in May is exquisite
on the outskirts of a village

350
大御油ひひなの殿にまゐらするわが前髪に桃の花ちる

ōmiabura
hiina no tono ni
mairasuru
waga maegami ni
momo no hana chiru

offering a light
at the palace of dolls
I pay homage
on the top of my hair
peach blossoms fall

351
夏花に多くの恋をゆるせしを神悔い泣くか枯野ふく風

natsubana ni
ōkuno koi wo
yuruseshi wo
kami kui naku ka
kareno fuku kaze

summer flowers
with so very much love
do the gods allow
a cry of regret as wind
blows over withered fields

352
道を云はず後を思はず名を問はずここに恋ひ恋ふ君と我と見る

michi wo iwazu
nochi wo omowazu
na wo towazu
koko ni koi kou
kimi to ware to miru

not preaching
not thinking of the future
nor asking for fame
here I only see
you and I in love

Myōjō, March, 1901.

353
魔に向ふつるぎの束をにぎるには細き五つの御指と吸ひぬ

ma ni mukoo
tsurugi no tsuka wo
nigiru ni wa
hosoki itsutsu no
miyubi to suinu

against the devil
your five fingers
are too slender
to seize the hilt of sword
I kissed them

354

消えむものか歌よむ人の夢とそはそは夢ならむさて消えむものか

kien monoka
uta yomu hito no
yume to so wa
so wa yume naran
sate kien mono ka

will it vanish
a poem chanted by someone
in a dream
one who even now has
disappeared from life

Myōjō, March, 1901.

355

恋と云はじそのまぼろしのあまき夢詩人もありき画だくみも
ありき

koi to iwaji
sono maboroshi no
amaki yume
shijin mo ariki
edakumi mo ariki

don't call it love
those sweet dreams
of illusion
there was a poet
then also a painter

356
君さけぶ道のひかりの遠を見ずやおなじ紅なる靄たちのぼる

kimi sakebu
michi no hikari no
ochi wo mizuya
onaji akenaru
moya tachinoboru

> you shout
> about the moral life
> don't you see
> beyond them rises
> a scarlet mist

357
かたちの子春の子血の子ほのほの子いまを自在の翅なからずや

katachi no ko
haru no ko chi no ko
honō no ko
ima wo jizai no
hane nakarazu ya

> a girl's beauty
> a girl in spring with a girl's blood
> is a girl's flame
> now how could I live
> without wings of freedom

When Akiko arrived in Tokyo to live with Tekkan life was not as glorious as she had dreamed. The housemaid, who liked Takino, gossiped against her. Her brothers were demanding she return home to take care of the family business so they would not have to. Even Tekkan's writing friends were against her.
Myōjō, July, 1901.

358

ふとそれより花に色なき春となりぬ疑ひの神まどはしの神

futo soreyori
hana ni iro naki
haru to narinu
utagai no kami
madowashi no
kami

suddenly since then
flowers have lost color
in spring
due to a god of doubt
a god of delusion

359

うしや我れさむるさだめの夢を永久にさめなと祈る人の子に
おちぬ

ushi ya ware
samuru sadame no
yume wo towa ni
sameruna to inoru
hito no ko ni ochinu

I am trying
to wake from the doomed
dream of forever
praying I won't awake
as a human child

360
わかき子が髪のしづくの草に凝りて蝶とうまれしここ春の国

wakaki ko ga
kami no shizuku no
kusa ni korite
chō to umareshi
koko haru no kuni

       a young girl
   water drips from her hair
     in the grass
   it changes into a butterfly
  here in the land of spring

Myōjō, July, 1901.

361
結願のゆふべの雨に花ぞ黒き五尺こちたき髪かるうなりぬ

kechigan no
yūbe no ame ni
hana zo kuroki
go-shaku kochitaki
kami karū narinu

   the prayer fulfilled
   in the evening rain
    are black flowers
  thick hair five feet long
     becomes light

Kechigan = prayer fulfilled is the last day of a period of prayers.

362

罪おほき男こらせと肌きよく黒髪ながくつくられし我

tsumi ooki
otoko korase to
hada kiyoku
kurokami nagaku
tsukurareshi ware

so many sins
to punish men
I was born
to have this fair skin
and long black hair

Myōjō, January, 1901.

363

そとぬけてその靄おちて人を見ず夕の鐘のかたへさびしき

so to nukete
sono moya ochite
hito wo mizu
yūbe no kane no
katae sabishiki

slipping out quietly
through the descended haze
I could not see anyone
how lonely is an evening
on one side of a bell

364
春の小川うれしの夢に人遠き朝を絵の具の紅き流さむ

haru no ogawa
ureshi no yume ni
hito tōki
asa wo enogu no
akaki nagasa'n

          spring river
      so happy with a dream
    though you are far away
     I will paint the dawn
      by pouring on red

365
もろき虹の七色恋ふるちさき者よめでたからずや魔神の翼

moroki niji no
nanairo kouru
chisaki mono yo
medetakarazu ya
magami no tsubasa

     a fragile rainbow
   its seven colors loved
      by a little one
  would you not be happier
    with the wings of devils

366

酔に泣くをとめに見ませ春の神男の舌のなにかするどき

> yoi ni naku
> otome ni mimase
> haru no kami
> otoko no shita no
> nanika surudoki

> a weeping drunk
> *young girl would you see*
> *a spring god*
> for a man's tongue
> it is somewhat sharp

367

その酒の濃きあぢはひを歌ふべき身なり君なり春のおもひ子

> sono sake no
> koki ajiwai wo
> utaubeki
> mi nari kimi nari
> haru no omoigo

> that wine
> of strong flavor
> you should make
> a poem of it yourself
> my beloved one in spring

368
花にそむきダビデの歌を誦せむにはあまりに若き我身とぞ思ふ

hana ni somuki
dabide no uta wo
zuse'n ni wa
amari ni wakaki
wagami to zo omou

having to recite
the Psalms of David
so unlike my life
I think I am
much too young

369
みかへりのそれはた更につらかりき闇におぼめく山吹垣根

mikaeri no
sore hata sarani
tsurakariki
yami ni obomeku
yamabuki kakine

looking back
it was much more
painful
to see a mountain rose hedge
looming in the dark

370
ゆく水に柳に春ぞなつかしき思はれ人に外ならぬ我

yuku mizu ni
yanagi ni haru zo
natsukashiki
omowarebito ni
hokanaranu ware

flowing water
and willows in spring
how dear these are
I am beloved
no less than they are

371
その夜かの夜よわきためいきせまりし夜琴にかぞふる三とせ
は長き

sono yo kano yo
yowaki tameiki
semarishi yo
koto ni kazouru
mitose wa nagaki

that night, the other night
the night when a soft sigh
closed down
counting on the harp
three years are long

372
きけな神恋はすみれの紫にゆふべの春の讃嘆のこゑ

kikena kami
koi wa sumire no
murasaki ni
yūbe no haru no
santan no koe

please listen god
love is a violet
purple
on a spring evening
the voice of wonder

373
病みませるうなじに繊きかひな巻きて熱にかわける御口を吸はむ

yamimaseru
unaji ni hosoki
kaina makite
netsu ni kawakeru
mikuchi wo suwa'n

since you are ill
I'll wrap around your neck
my slender arms
to suck your mouth
so dry from fever

Though the word *suwa'n* is usually translated as kiss the term suck is more accurate.

374

天の川そひねの床のとばりごしに星のわかれをすかし見るかな

amanogawa
soine no toko no
tobari goshi ni
hoshi no wakare wo
sukashi miru kana

in the Milky Way
through the curtains of the bed
where we sleep together
I see the morning parting
of those two stars

This refers to the Tanabata legend. In Japanese, *amanogawa* – river of heaven is the Milky Way.

375

染めてよと君がみもとへおくりやりし扇かへらず風秋となりぬ

somete yo to
kimi ga mimoto e
okuriyarishi
ōgi kaerazu
kaze aki to narinu

draw something
on this fan I have
sent to you
it has not yet come back
maybe it's the autumn wind

In a letter from Akiko to Tekkan when he was ill in Tokyo in Sepember, 1900. Poem was second in a series of 16 in *Myōjō*, September, 1900.

376
たまはりしうす紫の名なし草うすきゆかりを歎きつつ死なむ

tamawarishi
usumurasaki no
nanashigusa
usuki yukari wo
nagekitsutsu shinan

                    you gave me
                  a light purple
                 nameless grass
           grieving the fragile bond
                with it I will die

Also in the letter from Akiko to Tekkan in September, 1900 when he was
ill. This tanka was ninth in the series of sixteen.
Myōjō, September, 1900.

377
うき身朝をはなれがたなの細柱たまはる梅の歌ことたらぬ

ukimi asa wo
hanaregatana no
hosobashira
tamawaru ume no
uta kototaranu

                    my life is hard
               so I hate to part in the morning
                  from a slender pillar
           though you gave me a poem of plum
                   it is not enough

378

さおぼさずや宵の火かげの長き歌かたみに詞あまり多かりき

sa obosazuya
yoi no hokage no
nagaki uta
katami ni kotoba
amari ookariki

don't you think
that in the evening firelight
those long poems
we gave each other
had too many words

379

その歌を誦します声にさめし朝なでよの櫛の人はづかしき

sono uta wo
zushimasu koe ni
sameshi asa
nadeyo no kushi no
hito hazukashiki

the voice
reciting the poem
woke me at dawn
comb your hair
I was so ashamed

380
明日を思ひ明日の今おもひ宿の戸に倚る子やよわき梅暮れそめぬ

asu wo omoi
asu no ima omoi
yado no to ni
yoru ko ya yowaki
ume kuresomenu

thinking of tomorrow
of this moment tomorrow
on the door of an inn
I lean helplessly
as darkness starts over the plum

381
金色の翅あるわらは躑躅くはへ小舟こぎくるうつくしき川

konjiki no
hane aru warawa
tsutsuji kuwae
obune kogikuru
utsukushiki kawa

with golden wings
a boy holds an azalea
in his mouth
comes rowing a small boat
down a beautiful river

Myōjō, July, 1901.

382

月こよひいたみの眉はてらさざるに琵琶だく人の年とひますな

tsuki koyoi
itami no mayu wa
terasazaru ni
biwa daku hito no
toshi toi masuna

by the moon tonight
the wrinkled forehead
is not lighted
if so don't ask the age
of the one holding a lute

383

恋をわれ もろしと知りぬ別れかねおさへし袂風の吹きし時

koi wo ware
moroshi to shirinu
wakare kane
osaeshi tamoto
kaze no fukishi toki

love I
know is fragile
it's so hard to part
I had to hold his sleeve
when the wind blew

384

星の夜のむくのしらぎぬかばかりに染めしは誰のとがとおぼすぞ

hoshi no yo no
muku no shiraginu
kabakarini
someshi wa dare no
toga to obosuzo

stars at night
pure as white silk
like this
I have been dyed
whose fault is it

385

わかき子のこがれよりしは鑿のにほひ美妙の御相けふ身にしみぬ

wakaki ko no
kogare yorishi wa
nomi no nioi
mimyō no misō
kyō mi ni shiminu

as a young girl
I loved the fame
of the sculptor
now it is the beauty
that pierces my body

386

清し高しさはいへさびし白銀のしろきほのほと人の集見し
（酔茗の君の詩集に）

kiyoshi takashi
sawaie sabishi
shirogane no
siroki honō to
hito no shū mishi

pure magnificence
even if you say you are lonely
in the silver white
I saw the white-hot flame
of your book of poems

(for the book by Suimei)

Suimei was Kawai Suimei – a poet contemporary with Akiko and the
editor of the magazine *Kansai Bungaku*.

387

雁よそよわがさびしきは南なりのこりの恋のよしなき朝夕

kari yo so yo
waga sabishiki wa
minami nari
nokori no koi no
yoshinaki asayū

listen wild goose
my loneliness here
in the south
with only the remains of love
makes night and day useless

388

来し秋の何に似たるのわが命せましちひさし萩よ紫苑よ

kishi aki no
nani ni nitaru no
waga inochi
semashi chiisashi
hagi yo shion yo

> coming in autumn
> what is it that resembles
> my life
> something small and narrow
> like the bush clover or asters

389

柳あをき堤にいつか立つや我れ水はさばかり流とからず

yanagi aoki
tsutsumi ni itsuka
tatsu ya ware
mizu wa sabakari
nagare tokarazu

> green willows
> on the bank someday
> I can stand
> by the water like this when
> the current is not so fast

221

390

幸おはせ羽やはらかき鳩とらへ罪ただしたる高き君たち

sachi owase
hane yawarakaki
hato torae
tsumi tadashitaru
takaki kimitachi

please be happy
with the soft feathers you've pulled
from the dove
your sins are absolved
you dignified persons

391

打ちますにしろがねの鞭うつくしき愚かよ泣くか名にうとき羊

uchimasu ni
shirogane no muchi
utsukushiki
oroka yo naku ka
na ni utoki hitsuji

to strike
with a silver whip
is beautiful
it is foolish to cry for fame
if one is only a nameless sheep

392
誰に似むのおもひ問はれし春ひねもすやは肌もゆる血のけに
泣きぬ

dare ni nin no
omoi towareshi
haru hinemosu
yawahada moyuru
chinoke ni nakinu

you asked me
who is like the one you love?
in spring
all day long my skin burned
my blushes made me cry

393
庫裏の藤に春ゆく宵のものぐるひ御経のいのちうつつをかしき

kuri no fuji ni
haru yuku yoi no
monogurui
mikyō no inochi
utsutsu okashiki

under temple wisteria
on an evening late in spring
someone insane
recites a sutra
life really is beautiful

394
春の虹ねりのくけ紐たぐります羞ひ神の暁のかをりよ

haru no niji
neri no kukehimo
tagurimasu
hajiroi gami no
ake no kaori yo

spring rainbow
the pure silk cord
pulled
by a shy god
the dawn of fragrance

395
室の神に御肩かけつつひれふしぬゑんじなればの宵の一襲

muro no kami ni
mikata kaketsutsu
hirefushinu
enji nareba no
yoi no hitokasane

god of a bedroom
putting it on his shoulders
I kneeled down
as dark red as the robe
one wears in the evening

396

天の才ここににほひのうつくしき春をゆふべに集ゆるさずや

ame no sai
kokoni nioi no
utsukushiki
haru wo yūbe ni
shū yurusazu ya

> genius
> here the fragrance
> is beautiful
> on a spring evening I agree
> about the collected poems

397

消えて凝りて石と成らむの白桔梗秋の野生の趣味さて問ふな

kiete korite
ishi to naran no
shiro gikyō
aki no no-oi no
shumi sate touna

> vanishing
> to turn into the stone
> I am white bush clover
> wild in the autumn field
> don't ask me if I like it

398
歌の手に葡萄をぬすむ子の髪のやはらかいかな虹のあさあけ

uta no te ni
budō wo nusumu
ko no kami no
yawarakai kana
niji no asa-ake

in the poet's hand
the hair of the girl
who stole a grape
it is so very soft
a rainbow at dawn

399
そと秘めし春のゆふべのちさき夢はぐれさせつる十三弦よ

soto himeshi
haru no yūbe no
chisaki yume
haguresasetsuru
jūsangen yo

quietly hidden
in an evening of spring
a small dream
was lead off course
by the harp's 13 strings

INDEX OF FIRST LINES IN JAPANESE

TRANSLATORS

Machiko Kobayashi was born in 1939. She graduated from the Aoyama Gakuin University in Tokyo with a Bachelor's Degree in English and American Literature. She is now a Professor at the Babel University of Professional School of Translation. In her career she has translated 119 books of Harlequin Romance for Harlequin Japan Ltd. and four other novels with PHP Publishing, Kadokawa Books.

Ms. Kobayashi has studied tanka in the group, "Bilingual Tanka" and is a member of the Nihon Kajin Club and *The Tanka Journal*.

Jane Reichhold was born in Lima, Ohio, 1937. She moved to Hamburg, West Germany in 1971, when she married Werner Reichhold. Back in the States in 1987, she founded AHA Books Publishing Company, and the magazine *Mirrors International Haiku Forum*. She started the *Tanka Splendor* Awards in 1989, a contest which continued for twenty years. She was co-editor, with Werner Reichhold, of *Lynx*, a journal for linking poets with renga, ghazals, haibun, and tanka since 1993. The magazine has had an online presence since 2000 on AHA!poetry.com which Jane put on the Internet on December 7th, 1995.

Jane Reichhold was twice winner of the Museum of Haiku Literature Award in Tokyo and three-time winner of a Haiku Society of America Merit Book Award. She has published over forty books of tanka, renga, haiku and other poetry. This is her sixth book of translation.

In 1998 she was invited, with her husband, by the Imperial Family to attend the *Utakai Hajime* – The First Poetry Party of the Year at the Imperial Palace in the Pine Room. Four days later she was given, by command of Emperor Akihito, the sake bowl from which he had taken the ceremonial first sip of sake at a ceremony that day for her work with the tanka in English.

In 2010 she was invited by the PEN Club to speak on the topic of "Tanka" at the International PEN Congress in Tokyo, Japan on September, 27.

www.ingramcontent.com/pod-product-compliance
Lightning Source LLC
Chambersburg PA
CBHW051821090426
42736CB00011B/1590